STEVE MARX

CLOSE
LIKE
THE PROS

REPLACE WORN-OUT TACTICS
WITH THE POWERFUL STRATEGY OF
INTERACTIVE SELLING

CAREER
PRESS

Franklin Lakes, NJ

CLOSE LIKE THE PROS
Cover design by The DesignWorks Group

To order this title, please call toll-free 1-800-CAREER-1 (NJ and Canada: 201-848-0310) to order using VISA or MasterCard, or for further information on books from Career Press.

CAREER
PRESS

The Career Press, Inc., 3 Tice Road, PO Box 687,
Franklin Lakes, NJ 07417
www.careerpress.com

Library of Congress Cataloging-in-Publication Data

Available upon request.

ISBN-10: 1-56414-934-X
ISBN-13: 978-1-56414-934-3

ACKNOWLEDGMENTS

I didn't invent or create anything in this book. What I've brought to the subject is a long career fully immersed in sales and salespeople—many of them true pros—together with an eye, an ear, and a mind better tuned to strategy than most folks are blessed with. In other words, I've seen a lot of the same sales activity you have seen—though probably more of it—but I've been able to see it in a strategic framework, to place it into a system that makes sense, and to present it as a set of practices most anyone can understand and adopt. My company, The Center for Sales Strategy (CSS), has in turn taught the strategy of *interactive selling* to others; the CSS professional staff has witnessed, over and over, the impact interactive selling has on salespeople. So my first acknowledgement goes to the pros from whom I learned all of this; most of them couldn't *teach* me, but they sure could *show* me.

I acknowledge Peter Block, author of the seminal work on the consulting profession, *Flawless Consulting*, first published in 1980 and still going strong. Block first defined for me the practice of contracting, of managing expectations in a very purposeful and proactive manner, and I was able to quickly see that the world's best salespeople—themselves consultative by nature—were using contracting consistently and creatively. Again, most couldn't explain what they were doing, but Block did.

Few books are solely the work of one person. I am fortunate to have at CSS an extraordinarily talented group of associates, led by my senior partners, Jim Hopes and John Henley. Jim and John are gifted executives and leaders, trusted consultants and partners. Their support has been invaluable, especially during the many weeks consumed by writing the manuscript, during which I was available to them only rarely. Both helped midwife this book in ways too numerous to recount. Mike Anderson, Leslye Schumacher, Matt Sunshine, and Cindy Wheatley of CSS were of significant help in structuring, focusing, and sequencing the work, and in reviewing the manuscript. Brian Tomassetti of CSS contributed the graphics that brighten the book and illustrate some of the important concepts here.

I am indebted as well to those clients, friends, and associates who took time from their busy schedules and from their families to review the manuscript and suggest myriad improvements and enhancements. I thank Mitch Bentley, John Brejot, Jim Conlan, Jay O'Connor, Rich Nagel, Chris Redgrave, Evan Shepard, Anita Thomas, Howard Tuuri, and Ned Waugaman.

A range of CSS clients, former clients, and professional associates were kind enough to read the manuscript prior to publication and provide testimonials about the book and about interactive selling. I extend my thanks to Tony Alessandra, Carl Gardner, John Hayes, Dave Kennedy, Kimberly Rath, Patrick Sbarra, Marty Schaffel, Jon Schwartz, and Jim Zimmerman.

There are three people without whom this book surely would not exist at all. Steve Stockman urged me to stop merely talking about the project and start taking the steps toward making it a reality. Linda Stockman-Vines assisted immensely with an earlier, unpublished draft of the manuscript. Mark Wiskup, author of *Presentation SOS* and *The IT Factor*, showed me just how to prepare a formal nonfiction book proposal for agents and publishers. Mark introduced me to Bob Diforio of D4EO Literary Agency, whose contacts, knowledge, and influence run deep.

The team at Career Press was a delight to work with. Ron Fry has assembled a competent crew on whom I could rely to bring my vision for this book to life. I first met Michael Pye, acquisitions editor, followed later by Managing Editor Kristen Parkes; by Kara Reynolds, the editor of *Close Like the Pros*; and finally by Sales Manager Laurie Kelly-Pye. I thank them all for giving this project the care and attention it deserved, and for putting an excellent product into readers' hands, a work of which I am immensely proud.

A Website was established at *www.InteractiveSelling.com* to support the book and to support readers of the book, facilitating communication and networking about interactive selling. Web developments invariably involve a great many people filling specific roles, but development was ably led by Ed Mahusay and Charlie Marval; their team did a superb job.

Finally, my wife of 35-plus years, Merrill, makes everything I do easier and more worthwhile. Thank you, Merrill, for your patience, tolerance, support, and suggestions, and for your love and tuna-melt sandwiches that got me through some of the tougher writing days.

CONTENTS

SETTING EXPECTATIONS
What You Should Know Before Reading This Book

Who this book is for

Millions of people, in the United States alone, are employed in sales. They range from retail sales clerks and telemarketing representatives to sales executives whose smallest order runs well over a million dollars. No one book is ideal for all of them. *Interactive selling* is the strategy used by the most accomplished professionals in sales organizations that:

1. Sell to *other businesses*.
2. Expect to maintain an *ongoing relationship* with and to make future sales to its clients.

3. Sell *tailored solutions* developed from the company's portfolio of products, services, capabilities, and resources.

If those three characteristics describe the kind of selling you do, you'll enjoy reading *Close Like the Pros* because it zeroes in on your world, addresses your challenges, and gives you the tools to be the highly ethical and outrageously successful salesperson you've always wanted to be.

If you're in sales management, you'll discover here a system that's easily integrated into your existing sales processes, without altering existing structures and systems. In these pages you'll find insights that elude most salespeople, practices rarely spoken of by sales trainers, and a strategy that integrates your firm's selling and your customers' buying to achieve the kind of enduring client partnerships that have been the exception and can now become common.

WHAT THIS BOOK IS *NOT*

Unlike most other books on the sales shelf, *Close Like the Pros* does *not* present a total sales solution. Here you *won't* find an answer to every question you've ever had. This book is *not* an A-to-Z comprehensive selling system with forms, checklists, and templates. You don't need to dump everything you're doing now in order to adopt the strategy of interactive selling—you can simply stir it into the successful systems and practices you're using today.

My company, The Center for Sales Strategy, has been perfecting, teaching, implementing, practicing, and consulting on sophisticated and comprehensive *customer-focused* and *needs-based* selling systems since 1983. But I've written this book for all of you who *already* understand why and how you should focus on customer needs and let those needs provide the focus, power, and direction for your sale...those of you who have mastered the basics, but still want to grow, those of you who see the super-pros create powerfully strong client relationships and who want to deliver the kind of numbers they do. If that's not you, then put this book aside and first pick up any of the hundreds of books out there that delve deeply into assessing and responding to customer needs. *Close Like the Pros* moves beyond those basics, takes readers to the next level, and focuses only on how to make your sales process interactive.

How to read this book

I've designed this book to be as interactive as you would like it to be. If you want to get the full benefit of reading *Close Like the Pros*, you're going to have to do some of the lifting yourself! Interactive selling is a different way of thinking, a different way of working, a different way of *talking*. It doesn't require special talent, but as with other skills you've learned, it requires a little effort. I'll keep showing you how and offering examples of how the pros do it, but then it's your turn. In fact, peppered throughout the book are personal workshop segments I've called "Your Turn." In each one, I'll ask you to grab a pen or pencil, engage your brain, think about your clients, recall what you've learned in the prior pages, and write down exactly what you will do to put the practices of interactive selling to work. Getting into this groove requires that you ponder, plan, and practice; if you put in the practice *while you're reading* the book, you'll learn more, and you'll be closing like the pros all the sooner.

This book is interactive in another way: I welcome your comments and observations. Please e-mail me at SteveMarx@InteractiveSelling.com. I read every piece of mail I receive, and you just might find a reply in your inbox! I'm also maintaining a blog at *www.InteractiveSelling.com*, where you can interact with me and other readers.

WHY YOU DON'T HAVE TO HIDE THIS BOOK FROM YOUR CLIENTS AND PROSPECTS

This is one of the few books ever published about selling that you could actually *share* with your clients and prospects! Yes, you could show it to them, proudly! The pros don't abuse their clients, so there's nothing abusive in *Close Like the Pros*. Nearly every other book on the shelf (and nearly every other sales training program or seminar) is one you dare not mention to customers. You would be embarrassed to have a prospect see the way customers are described, and how those selling systems encourage their disciples to trick or trap the prospect into the sale. Worse yet, if a prospect read about those tactics, he'd be in on the joke and easily able to neutralize every gambit, outwit every ploy. There's nothing between the covers here that any clients or prospects shouldn't see—you might even want to buy them a copy!

WELCOME TO INTERACTIVE SELLING

You're about to become more powerful—by giving up power. For many readers, interactive selling is the last piece of the puzzle, the only thing standing between you and *closing like the pros!*

CHAPTER ONE
BURNED AGAIN BY HANDOFF SELLING

GRAND SPRINGS HEALTH WAS THE PERFECT PROSPECT. And you've just delivered the perfect proposal. You showed its senior purchasing managers you were in their corner, even before they placed the first order with you. It was a tremendous performance, as you knew it would be.

After all, you had jumped on inside information and sprung into action just as Grand Springs Health had identified its supply problem, but long before it had issued a request for proposal that would have invited all your competitors in too. What a golden opportunity! You asked all the right probing questions on your prior call. You logged the intense hours, did the research, and demonstrated some real sweat-equity in this future relationship. It took some perseverance, but you found a wealth of data online about Grand Springs Health—number of locations, number of physicians, major specialty areas, patient counts, and on and on. Together with what you learned on your earlier call from the assistant director of purchasing, you were able to perform a detailed analysis of Grand Springs Health's use of consumables and the four issues it seemed to have—quality, price, warehousing, and delivery. Everything fell together beautifully as you crafted a response that answered every one of the company's concerns—the kind of turnkey plan that's become your trademark. Your solution showed all the work you had put into the project, and your PowerPoint slides were not only on-target, they were handsome and polished.

On top of that, your presentation in their conference room could not have come off better, filled with just the right amount of intensity, confidence, friendliness, and persuasion. How could they not be impressed? They had to be, because you left no stone unturned. You could not have done more.

It was deflating and baffling when they didn't buy your proposal. Worse, it wasn't even a definitive no. Rather, it was a vague and almost patronizing "You did a nice job. We'll certainly keep you in mind as we move through the process." The marbles were on the table that day, but you didn't win even one. You didn't win, but neither is it clear whether or not you lost, or even whether a clear no would have been better than this non-outcome. Yes, you're in limbo—the oh-so-familiar limbo that follows more and more sales calls these days, the *what do I do now* limbo that follows most salespeople around throughout their career—and the longer the limbo lasts, the more you come to understand that the limbo is a lose.

The longer the limbo lasts, the more likely it's a lose.

Have you been in that movie?

Perhaps you should do less of the lifting

If you've been selling business-to-business services or solutions for more than five minutes, you've had that experience. We all have. It's not even the exception anymore. Some days, it seems to be the rule. It's frustrating, it's unnerving, and worst of all, it's puzzling. *What more could the prospect want? If it was my price, why didn't they at least say so? What am I missing? Why does this keep happening to me? I bust my butt to assemble an exceptional proposal, and I get a vague, lukewarm, nonresponse. It's not even a no. I could deal with it better if it was a no. Wait, what am I saying? I don't want to hear them say no. At least I'm still alive with this prospect, but what do I do now?*

Most salespeople are trying hard to do it right. They're painstakingly following the rules, the established protocol, and their specific company and industry "selling steps" to a tee. Yet day after day, month after month, proposal after proposal, they continue to hear the dreaded words: "Well, you've certainly given us a lot to think about. We'll be reviewing your proposal in the next quarter, and we'll get back to you." It's the equivalent of a 10th-grader being told, "You have a really great personality"—it means you're probably not going to the dance together. All the work, all the research, all the design, all the customization, all the competitive analysis you've done is down the drain.

It has never occurred to most salespeople that the key to success might be found in doing *less* of the lifting all by themselves. Instead, they keep on working in a vacuum, on a different track from the prospect, with disheartening results. The seller is on a selling track, the buyer is on a buying track, and they rarely intersect. It's true these are their respective job descriptions, but it's time to update those job descriptions. Selling and buying both become more efficient, productive, and successful when they are merged into a single *interactive* process.

As long as you stick to your selling track, you and your prospect are like two freight trains passing in the night. And *trying harder* makes your problem worse! The more focused you are on selling, the bigger the disconnect you have with the buyer. That's why there's still no purchase order with your company's name on it sitting in the buyer's outbox.

Trying harder makes your problem worse.

Selling isn't easy these days, if it ever was. *But neither is buying.* As business gets tougher and more competitive, as the choices on the market become more numerous and more complex, as the stakes are raised for everyone, buying decisions become more difficult. The more options there are, the more variables, the more vendors, the more channels, the more salespeople, the more hype...the more help buyers need. Every decision seems to be more complicated, with more moving parts and more people involved. These days, every purchase decision involves increased risk, and the bigger the price tag the greater the risk.

But the pattern continues. The prospect tells you she's busy and just needs your proposal or your bid, and you dutifully comply. She means no harm, and is probably as clueless as you are that her request to get your proposal ASAP is in neither her best interests nor yours. Because you're customer-needs-focused, and her professed need right now is for you to turn that bid around and submit it fast, you head back to the office fully focused on the task. Once in your cubicle, you set out to prove to the prospect how well you can perform without bugging her, how much you can know and do without consulting her, how much of the burden you're willing to lift from her shoulders and scratch from her to-do list.

THE PRESSURE COOKER WE LIVE IN

Among the reasons you're so willing to do so much for this prospect is that you empathize with her. Who knows more than you what it means to be crazy-busy? You live in a pressure cooker yourself. Let us count the ways:

You've got **competitive pressure**, as never before. Your toughest competitor used to be across the street; today it's across the globe. And the cross-town competitors haven't gone away either.

You've got **budget pressure**, each year steeper than the year before. You don't need to work for a large, publicly traded firm in order to feel the heat of constantly rising expectations and demands. Smaller companies are setting tougher goals too.

You've got **deadline pressure**. Your deadlines may be client-imposed, company-imposed, even self-imposed, and gone is the luxury of working on one deadline at a time.

You've got **corporate pressure** that goes well beyond hitting a budget number. The company just installed new software and expects you to master it. They sent you to a two-day training workshop last week and they expect to see evidence that you're applying what you learned.

You've got **boss pressure**. He's one pretty terrific guy, among the best you've ever worked for, and that's the problem. When he asks you to turn up the heat, to crank up the pace, to help the team power ahead, you just can't turn a deaf ear to that. Many a well-meaning boss (with his own pressures!) will urge you to turn the project around fast and get the proposal on the buyer's desk, clueless that there's no connection between a rapid turnaround and a big sale, or a good sale, *In most industries, there's no connection between a rapid turnaround and a good sale.* or a profitable sale, or a sale that's likely to turn into many more sales.

If you've got family, you've got *family pressure*. When you spend so much time at work, you feel guilty about spending so little time with your family. And when you're with your family, you feel guilty about not being at work.

You've got *financial pressure*. Because you're in sales, tomorrow's paycheck is unpredictable, but tomorrow's expenses are not. There are some fabulous months, and the occasional really good year, but you're familiar with the lean times as well, and fear of another keeps the pressure on.

You've got *client pressure*. As you've built your book of business, your client list has grown and grown. Every one of those clients has ongoing expectations, and some have constant demands. Sometimes it means new or increased business, but often meeting client demands simply ensures that existing business will continue.

And you've got *prospect pressure*. That's where our list started. Right or wrong, she wants your proposal on her desk by Monday morning, unaware that she's asking for your weakest work.

So many of the pressures we feel manifest themselves as *time pressure*. Regardless of how much time we invest, it seems as if it's never enough. We say *invest*, but when it comes to our sales job, we don't treat our precious hours with the same *investment mindset* with which we treat our precious dollars. Investment implies the notion of return, but salespeople the world over don't pay nearly enough attention to the return they're (not) getting on their often elaborate investment of time. Instead, most of us respond to time pressure by squeezing in more prospects, talking faster, skipping lunch, staying late (and later!), and collecting speeding tickets. It's the real-life equivalent of the classic *I Love Lucy* episode in which Lucy and Ethel decide to supplement their respective household incomes by taking jobs on the

> *Most salespeople don't treat their precious hours with the same investment paradigm with which they treat their precious dollars.*

assembly line in a candy factory. It's fine for the first few minutes, until the foreman starts to "speed things up a little." The faster the candy-ingredient belt moves, the bigger the mess. The scene ends in the typical *Lucy* slapstick farce, with supporting comedic performances by chocolate, nuts, and butter cream. There's not much slapstick in today's sales jobs, but there's too much farce as salespeople invest time without monitoring the return they're getting, indeed, without *modulating* their investment according to return.

Too much time working on the prospect, too little time working with the prospect.

Too often, sellers mistakenly respond to the myriad pressures and time challenges confronting them—and confronting their buyers—by spending more time alone, holed up in the office, working *on* the prospect instead of working *with* the prospect. It's the most fundamental mistake made by salespeople today. Salespeople get way out in front of their prospect, without ever checking the rearview mirror to see if the prospect is still following and just how closely. They over-prepare, believing all that prep to be an advantage (*sometimes* it is) and oblivious to the ways in which it hobbles their efforts, with both the prospect for whom they're over-preparing and all the other prospects for whom they are inevitably under-preparing. But this investment-without-return scenario continues, because it's what we've all been taught to do, trained to do, and told to do. We sit at our desks, put our heads down, and prepare like mad, because we have a lot to say, a lot to offer, a lot of capabilities that might bear on the prospect's circumstances, and a lot of fear that the next call will be an all-or-nothing event, our last shot. It amounts to what many a pundit has called *premature elaboration*, a condition as undesirable and ineffective as its namesake.

As a result, too often our hard work just goes to waste. Way too many deals simply don't happen. I've lost count of how many times a salesperson has told me, "If only I'd known the deal was headed nowhere, I would have cut my losses and moved on. I can't believe how much time and momentum I lost on that one piece of non-business." Whenever I hear stories similar to that, I flash back to my mom and the old expression she liked to repeat: *The hurrier I go, the behinder I get.* (And that was when I was just a kid! Hey, Mom, if you're listening up there, it's way worse today, worse by several orders of magnitude.) For most salespeople, interactive selling is a new way of working. You'll no longer feel as though you're on a fast track to nowhere. When you sell interactively, some of your prospects get stronger and healthier than would have been possible otherwise, and the rest show their weakness early on, so you can move on.

THE ILLUSION OF THE TWO-CALL CLOSE

No one in professional selling talks much about the *one-call close* anymore. That was the idea that really good salespeople could walk out with an order from their first-ever encounter with a prospect. Perhaps it was true in the quaint days of residential door-to-door selling, but it was rarely ever the case for those of us selling business services and solutions. What we hear instead, from a great many sales managers, is the *two-call close*. It too is an illusion, and a dangerous one at that. In fact, calling it the *two-call non-close* would bring us closer to reality about 97 percent of the time. I'll prove it to you.

Think about your own selling experiences. You assess needs on your first call, and you deliver a very workable, perhaps even highly attractive, solution on your second call. All is according to plan. You ask the prospect what he would like to do next, and what do you hear most often? "Yes, I'll take it"? Probably not. What you hear sounds closer to, "You've given me a lot to think about here. Give me some time...." And how could they respond any other way? Most people need time to think about things they are seeing for the first time.

Being the diligent salesperson you are, you ask the prospect when you should get back to him. "Next Tuesday." You call faithfully next Tuesday, and if you get through, you'll hear, "I gotta tell ya, since we talked last week, I've just been jammed. Haven't even had a chance to study that proposal," or, "You know, I sent it up to my boss, and he hasn't gotten back to me yet. As soon as I know something, I'll give you a call."

I know what happens next. You ask when you should get back to the prospect (inherently not relying on the prospect to call you). The prospect hesitates a bit, and asks for another 10 days "or so." That's twice as long as he asked for the first time, following your delivery of the proposal.

Dutifully, and again proving your reliability and punctuality, you call back on the 10th day. If he takes your call, what do you hear? If he really likes you, he apologizes; otherwise, he just moves directly into a request for more time and more patience. You might hear, "back burner," "other options," or "next quarter." Again, you inquire as to a good day or week to get back in touch, and you get a vague answer. You decide on your own to mark your calendar for three weeks hence.

You call back on the very day you wrote in your calendar and leave a voicemail in a half-hearted attempt to salvage your work and your investment. You've made five calls by this point, not two, and the last three have been lousy, empty, awkward calls that didn't have the positive, creative, forward-focused feel of those first two calls, the calls that came before you handed off the proposal.

The calls you make after handing off the proposal don't have the same value—for anyone—as the calls you make before.

It's not always this bad, of course. Sometimes you get the business! But it still takes five calls, or 12 calls, or whatever. Once the prospect studies your proposal, she's bound to have questions. "Thanks for calling. I had a question. I didn't understand the pricing method at all. Never seen that approach before." You take the opportunity to explain your novel pricing concept, and ask when you should call next. On the following call, you hear, "Yeah, my boss had a question. Rather than my trying to explain his question and then going back to him to explain your answer, I should just put you guys together. His number is 555-2368." Now you're playing telephone tag with the boss. You'll probably eventually hook up, and you may actually do business with them, but *two calls?* You know better! And your boss who talks up the two-call close? He's dreaming...been off the street too long.

INTERACTIVE SELLING HARBORS NO ILLUSIONS

Interactive selling is founded on the notion that the two-call close is the great exception, not the typical case. Selling interactively means you assume there will be lots of back and forth, lots of give and take, lots of questions and answers, lots of modifying and tweaking—and you've designed your sales approach around the natural way real people actually work. Interactive selling simply *relocates* the delivery of the formal proposal to the end of the process, and that suddenly, almost miraculously, *lights up* all those calls beyond the second call, converting them from the empty, awkward, "So, any news yet on my proposal?" to active, problem-solving, partnership-molding calls. These are calls the prospect takes every time because it's a worthwhile and helpful call, because she's making an important contribution to the project, and because the proposal isn't complete yet!

Interactive selling relocates the delivery of the formal proposal.

Here's how it works in practice: Instead of going off into your isolation chamber to work on a solution by yourself, you know the prospect is as close as your phone and your e-mail, and quite possibly another in-person visit or two. As you look through your notes from that first call, you realize you're not entirely sure you fully understood the differences between the work flow procedures for their office staff and for their telecommuting staff. You're also thinking about a few other questions you wish you'd have thought to ask. So you pick up the phone. The prospect appreciates your interest and your diligence, and is delighted to provide more information if it will improve the proposal she's seeking. Based on the nature of this call, she's more likely to take your next call. You let her know you'll be getting back to her soon to run several possible approaches by her. Before that day even arrives, you've had two other brief e-mail exchanges with her.

A week later, you're face-to-face in her office again, sharing several concepts and approaches, and seeking her input on each. She shoots one down, has a tepid reaction to another, but is smiling and highly engaged when speaking about the third possibility. You ask more questions about all three, even the dead-on-arrival idea, because every answer gives you more information about her needs and her decision-making criteria, information that will sharpen your proposal and put your competitors at a severe disadvantage. (You're thanking yourself for having brought these possibilities to her in raw form, because otherwise you were likely to have built out your first concept, the one she couldn't possibly have bought for reasons you could not have known.) Now you've got the prospect leaning forward, actively participating, and suggesting how your third concept would need to be adapted in order to work for her company. *It's as if she's helping you write your proposal!* You're taking notes and doing a little brainstorming on the spot. You set a day and time to get back to her with something on paper.

Back at the office, you're investing more time, confident that you see a likelihood of substantial return. Another phone call and three more e-mail exchanges ensue before you're finally ready to reveal your recommendations in the form of a proposal.

By the time you're in front of her again, it's your fourth face-to-face meeting and your 10th interaction, counting phone calls and e-mails. The big difference is that you focused not only on your selling, but equally on her buying. You were determined not to offer a plan this prospect couldn't or wouldn't buy, and not to leave all the trouble-shooting and repairing until after you had delivered the formal proposal, understanding that there would be no assurance you'd ever get back in to trouble-shoot and repair. In other words, you were selling *interactively.* And the prospect responded accordingly. She was buying, one step at a time, while you were selling. She was investing time and energy in proportion to yours. She knew what was in your proposal before you delivered it, and she was eager to buy your proposal before she could even hold it in her hands. It was as if she coauthored the proposal, and in many ways, she had. So it was no surprise she said yes that very day, or soon thereafter. You were closing like a pro!

Focus not only on your selling, but equally on their buying.

THE HANDOFF SELLING MODEL DOESN'T WORK

Your earlier *two-call-close* attempt did put a proposal in the prospect's hands in one week flat, but the process still consumed five calls over six weeks before fading into oblivion, before you quietly deleted it from your list of pending business. Contrast that with your *interactive* approach: It consumed 10 calls and exchanges over just three weeks, synchronized the buying process with the selling process, and resulted in a proposal that was buyable the very day it was delivered. *You got a faster—and better—answer with a slower proposal.*

Interactive selling doesn't guarantee every sale will be made; that kind of outcome is reserved for magic shows. But every interactive seller out there will attest that the process puts the wind at his back instead of in his face, because *interactive selling improves both the proposal and the prospect.* Interactive selling makes the prospect an active participant in the selling phase and the salesperson an active participant in the buying phase. Indeed, when an interactive seller is on the scene, no observer could identify what parts of the dialogue are selling and what parts are buying; sometimes, it's even tough for a fly on the wall to tell who's the seller and who's the buyer!

The rapidly delivered proposal is based on a concept I call *handoff selling,* an approach that's almost ubiquitous today, at company after company, in industry after industry. The monkey is on the salesperson's back right up until the handoff. Then the baton—the proposal—is handed off, as if this were a high school relay race, and the sales rep falls away and trots off the track. The seller who works this way has finished her work when she delivers the proposal. At that moment, the monkey jumps onto the prospect's back because the selling process is over and the buying process is about to begin. The salesperson has nothing more to say, no role left to play, no right to expect even that her phone calls will be returned unless the buyer happens to have a question.

Delivering the final proposal is like passing the baton in a relay race—your role is over.

This kind of handoff selling benefits neither seller nor client. The buyer is remarkably uninvolved in the selling phase, except to answer a few perfunctory questions. And worse, the seller is not involved in the buying process—not there to help, not there to problem-solve, not there to steer the outcome toward a win-win. Half the transaction, of course, is *buying,* and the seller is not even in the room!

There's no handoff in interactive selling. To maintain the metaphor, we could say that both salesperson and prospect have one hand on the baton from the moment the starting gun is heard and all the way to the tape at the finish line (and beyond).

Handoff Selling

HANDOFF   DECISION
(proposal delivered)

Interactive Selling

DECISION
(proposal delivered)

The interactive seller understands the importance of both halves of the transaction, takes it upon herself to synchronize them into a single process, and gets her prospect to be her partner from the very outset. The interactive salesperson recognizes that the big decision at the end of the process—the one the seller sweats and the buyer dreads—can be broken down into a *series* of decisions, of narrowing the options, of rejecting some possibilities and embracing others...a series of logical, sequential, incremental, progressive, mini-decisions taken together by the buyer and the seller. In doing so, the interactive seller has reached the zenith of her profession: She has *gotten the prospect involved to improve the selling process* and she has *gotten herself involved to improve the buying process*. The outcome is almost invariably better for both parties.

> *Every big decision is really the result of a series of logical, sequential, incremental, mini-decisions.*

THE TIME IS RIGHT FOR INTERACTIVE SELLING

There are some significant trends in society and in business that make interactive selling especially urgent right now for nearly every professional selling organization:

Mass customization alters buyer expectations. Instead of buying a computer off the shelf, many consumers opt to visit Websites where they configure their machine with precisely the features and capabilities that best serve their needs. This desire for individualized products and solutions is not limited to high-tech, high-ticket items: Consumers are now able to configure their own jeans, and the factory makes them and ships them. Today, we expect to find *exactly* what we're looking for, even if that means it must be built from scratch. We expect to have at least some influence over the design of the products and services we buy. As buyers, we expect more than choice—we expect to be catered to.

It's ironic that millions of salespeople today, sitting face-to-face with their prospect, are less solicitous of and less receptive to input than are many Websites! Interactive selling is built on the premise that the prospect wants to and should play a significant role in developing the proposal or plan he is offered. **Individuals are empowered as never before.** *TIME Magazine* writer Lev Grossman put it simply and powerfully (March 12, 2006): "The authorship of innovation is shifting from the Few to the Many." Increasingly, people are expecting to be involved in creating, collaborating on, customizing, or configuring the solutions and systems they use. If there is a developmental process going on behind that door, they expect the door to be opened to them, so they can at least watch, if not tweak, twist, or even tear apart. More and more, each of us is a *participant*, not a spectator, in the tailoring of our world, including our world at work.

The salespeople who are winning biggest now are those who understand that they gain power when they empower others. The salespeople who rise to the top will be those who recognize that their prospects now have the power not just to choose which product, service, or solution they'll buy, but to help craft it as well. They'll use interactive selling to share power, control, and decision-making...in both directions.

You gain power when you empower others.

Collaboration is no longer novel; it's the norm. Formalized joint ventures between organizations are nothing new. What is new, compelling, and dramatically different is how commonplace collaboration has become in today's flat, informal, and nonhierarchical business organizations. In his best-selling book, *The World is Flat*, Thomas Friedman writes, "...it is now possible for more people than ever to collaborate and compete in real time with more other people on more different kinds of works from more different corners of the planet on a more equal footing than at any previous time in the history of the world...." New expectations and new technology are making peers of nearly everyone: individuals as well as their companies, intra-company collaborators and inter-company collaborators, brief collaborators and durable collaborators, full collaborators and partial collaborators, even competitor-collaborators who never before thought they'd even say hello if they ran into each other on the street. Friedman calls this the evolution from "command and control" to "collaborate and connect."

The now common expectation of close collaboration, and the high degree of interactivity required for it, is causing companies to shorten their list of vendors and suppliers, and to deepen and strengthen their ties with those that remain. Too many salespeople still look and act as though they're stuck in the command-and-control world of the past. Salespeople who are not connecting and collaborating with their clients—to whatever extent may be appropriate given their product or service—will be passed by in favor of those who are.

Wiki wiki: **Technology makes it easy and fast.** Collaborative software and work flow applications are changing our work just as much as word-processing software did in the last century. These are the engines without which the drive for intense collaboration and individual empowerment would be difficult to fulfill. At the forefront of collaborative technology are Web-based *wikis* ("wickies"), group-editable Web pages that are typical of the movement toward royalty-free, nearly cost-free, open-source software.

Online collaboration can be expected to infiltrate nearly every process in business (and beyond), including your sales interactions and your client-solution development projects. These 21st century ways of doing business require interactive selling. *Wiki* is Hawaiian for "quick" or "fast." *Wiki wiki* is faster still. Collaboration need neither be complex nor time consuming; indeed, it's used today to speed products to market, not to delay them. Interactive salespeople who slow down and take the time to collaborate will get the order *wiki wiki*!

Openness and transparency are no longer optional. Business is no longer a black-box operation. Transparency is replacing what once happened behind closed doors. It's not only government agencies conforming to the Freedom of Information Act, nor public companies falling in line with the requirements of Sarbanes-Oxley. It's a general push away from anything about which the customer might be suspicious merely because it's out of sight.

Today we expect everything to be above-board, full-disclosure, out-on-the-table. We want the straight poop when we read the ingredients on a food-product label, when we use our favorite search engine online, and when there's a salesman sitting across the table from us. Interactive selling is for salespeople with nothing to hide. Rather than concealing the process, it opens it up.

Hype and spin don't work the way they used to. People younger than 35, and a great many who are older, seem to have been born with a BS-meter that detects hype, and a BS-buzzer that goes off every time they see or hear it. The most effective TV commercials once were those that shouted the most outrageous claims; today it's the ones whispering simple truths. Consumers are more likely now to trust a plain-text, six-word ad sitting adjacent to search-engine results than an overproduced ad campaign. And they'll trust user reviews and unbiased comparisons more than what they hear from the typical salesperson. The steak is emerging from behind the sizzle.

Interactive selling puts the quiet power of underselling to work.

The era of slickness and hype, of clever spinmeistering, of the fancy two-step and the smooth gloss-over is largely behind us. With interactive selling, you put the quiet power of underselling to work, and there are no questions of trust. The whole process is *real*, and everyone reaps the rewards.

More decision-influencers have a say. Empowerment, collaboration, complexity, risk—they have all played a part in producing an ever-increasing number of decision-influencers, people who are listened to, and often heeded, before the decision is made. Few substantial decisions are made these days before getting the stamp of approval from one or more committee, task force, ad hoc group, or self-directed team. The *interactive seller* uses specific tools to keep every stakeholder engaged.

The cost of an in-person sales call continues to zoom. Many organizations today calculate the cost of the average face-to-face sales call in the hundreds of dollars, and when that call involves travel, sometimes the thousands of dollars. If a call leads to good business, it's a good investment. But if it leads to a dead end, it is a very expensive loss. Smart sales organizations qualify prospects in advance to limit the number of calls made on prospects who are unlikely to buy, but that's no longer enough. Interactive selling provides *continuous qualification* of the prospect, so the salesperson can modulate his investment of time and resources, focusing only where he's most likely to see a return.

The digitizing of communication adds new risks. Gone are the days when most client contact was face-to-face. Now, clients expect to interact with us through e-mail, instant messaging, conference calls, groupware, and Web conferencing, not to mention phone, fax, and voice mail. Although these tools enhance communication in valuable ways, they also increase the risk of miscommunication, misunderstanding, and missteps. When we meet in person, we have three channels of communication operating: the verbal (our words), the visual (our facial animations and body language), and the vocal (our tone and inflection). When our communication goes digital, three

Digital adds danger: Three channels of communication are reduced to two, and often just one.

channels are reduced to two, and often just one. Interactive selling helps you manage expectations—whatever the medium, whatever the channel—more closely and carefully, to avoid running projects off the path and into the ditch.

WELCOME TO INTERACTIVE SELLING

If you believe your only big selling problem is closing, that everything sails along smoothly for you until it's time for The Close, you're probably using the wrong definition of closing. You've probably tried all those worn-out closing tactics—the Ben Franklin Close, the Puppy Dog Close, and the Think It Over Close; the Porcupine Close and the Hot Potato Close; and let us not forget the First-One-to-Talk-Loses Close and of course, the *Reductio Ad Absurdum* Close. Those tried-and-false closes reveal the truth: Your problem is not in front of you; *it's behind you.*

By the time you're ready to confirm the order, to get that signature, The Close should not be your last big step. If you want to close like the pros, you'll have accomplished most—nearly all—of the closing process *before* the day the prospect actually signs the deal. That's what interactive selling does for you. Just as the smart way to eat an elephant is "one bite at a time," so too the smart way to close business is *one increment at a time.* If you know that the old definition of closing is stale, if you understand that the old tricks of closing are dead, then you're ready to transition your sales approach to interactive selling. Closing is important, but the way the *pros* close is the very antithesis of the sleazy closing tactics that have given most salespeople a shaky reputation.

Now that you've seen the difference between an interactive selling pro and a sleazy salesman, you're ready to discover a whole new way of thinking about your job. I'll explain the two fundamental practices that form the foundation of interactive selling:

⊙ Contracting—The management of expectations.

⊙ Partnering—The sharing of control, decision-making, and accountability.

I'll introduce you to a new language to describe your new way of thinking about your job:

⊙ Ground rules.

⊙ Clear paths and genuine agendas.

⊙ Mini-closes.

⊙ Molehill decisions.

⊙ Homework assignments.

⊙ Half-baked ideas.

⊙ Trial balloons.

⊙ Progress reports.

⊙ No-surprise proposal.

⊙ Critical path.

⊙ Post-sale partner.

Welcome to interactive selling, *where you and the prospect, working together, create a better proposal—and where you and the proposal, working together, create a better prospect.*

CLOSING THE CHAPTER

I believe these are some of the key takeaways from this chapter:

⊙ Selling is tough, but so is buying. Both become more effective and productive when they're merged into a single interactive process.

⊙ Most salespeople spend too much time working *on* the prospect, and too little time working *with* the prospect.

⊙ Over and over, salespeople invest too much time in prospects who are unlikely to buy, and too little time in those who will.

- The two-call close is an illusion, spoken of seriously only by idealistic sales trainers and pressured sales managers.

- *Handoff selling* guarantees only that you won't be around while your prospect investigates the issues, deals with the details, and crunches the numbers.

- The time is right for *interactive selling.*

- The prospect can help you improve the proposal, and the proposal can help you improve the prospect.

What were the most important points to remember—from your perspective? What passages did you underline or highlight? I'd love to know. E-mail me at SteveMarx@InteractiveSelling.com and include "Chapter 1" in your subject line.

CHAPTER TWO

STOP NEGLECTING HALF YOUR JOB

ARE YOU AN INTERACTIVE SALESPERSON ALREADY?

In your heart, you want to do the right thing. You do an exhaustive needs analysis to ensure you understand what the prospect wants to accomplish. You pore over your proposal, aiming to polish and perfect it. You make every effort to price your product in such a way that it's a good value for the client and still a profitable deal for your company. You sweat the details. You're genuinely concerned about your customers and you treat your accounts to an outstanding level of service. But is that enough? Does that make you an *interactive seller*?

YOUR TURN

You may be wondering just how well you practice *interactive selling* already. The following Self-Assessment Survey will help you figure that out. You may complete it by writing your answers right here in the pages of this book, or if you prefer, you can visit *www.InteractiveSelling.com* and complete the survey—free— online. Many people will find it more fun and easier to do it online. When you complete the survey online, the Website does all the work of calculating your answers.

Read all three statements in each group before answering. Then select the *one with which you identify the most* and place a **3** in the box to the left of the letter. Next, choose the statement *with which you identify least* and place a **1** to the left of it. Finally, place a **2** to the left of the remaining statement.

Be honest and candid with yourself. You may be able to tell from the context which is probably the best *interactive selling* answer, but you won't learn much about your own approach to selling—and how interactive you really are—unless you place that **3** next to the statement that truly reflects how *you* think and act *most of the time*. Think back to the actual selling situations you've been in the last week, the last month, even the last year.

SELF-ASSESSMENT SURVEY

GROUP 1

☐ **A** I've found it's best to let the prospect take the call in whichever direction he or she prefers.

☐ **B** I believe in keeping control of the sales process—I run it in such a way as to ensure that I meet my objectives.

☐ **C** For me, control is a shared responsibility; together we decide how to spend our time and which way to take the conversation.

GROUP 2

☐ **A** Sales is a numbers game. If you want to make your numbers, you gotta keep the pressure on—more pavement, more prospects, more pitches.

☐ **B** I understand that sales is a numbers game. That's why I get in front of as many people as possible.

☐ **C** Sales isn't really a numbers game! I turn the odds in my favor by investing my time and effort with prospects who are responding.

GROUP 3

☐ **A** Even early in the sales cycle, I'm starting to get a pretty good handle on whether we'll be doing business or not.

☐ **B** I'm highly responsive to every prospect. Of course, I'm hoping there'll be an order at the end of the process, but I'm also prepared for the worst.

☐ **C** I go all out, but it's tough to tell in advance who'll say yes and who won't.

GROUP 4

☐ **A** If I encounter an awkward moment on a sales call—say, the prospect is getting confused or suspicious about something—I just smooth it over and carry on.

☐ **B** Awkward moments are few and far between, because my prospects always know where we're heading in the call; in fact, they've agreed to it in advance.

☐ **C** I dread those awkward moments with a prospect; they don't happen all that often, but when they do, I just back off.

GROUP 5

☐ **A** My prospects learn pretty quickly that they can trust me to deliver exactly what they asked for.

☐ **B** Prospects are naturally suspicious of salespeople, but I don't let that slow me down. They'll trust me more, once we're doing business.

☐ **C** It's amazing how quickly trust builds between my prospects and me. I think they naturally trust me when they see that I trust them.

GROUP 6

☐ **A** Getting a handle on the client's needs is something neither she nor I can do alone.

☐ **B** Nobody knows the client's needs better than the client; I let her fill me in.

☐ **C** Frankly, I usually have the client's needs figured out before she does!

GROUP 7

☐ **A** I find it best to support the client's ideas and solutions.

☐ **B** There's a lot of give and take—both the client and I contribute essential elements to the solution.

☐ **C** Knowing my products and services as well as I do, I can put together a package without taking much of the client's time.

GROUP 8

☐ **A** I respond quickly—I nearly always have my proposal ready for our second appointment.

☐ **B** I'll have a proposal ready for our second meeting, unless the prospect indicates otherwise.

☐ **C** My proposals take a while; typically they come together after a number of meetings, e-mails, and phone calls.

GROUP 9

☐ **A** My prospects do as much or as little work to develop the plan as they wish to do. Often they know exactly what they want, which makes things a lot easier.

☐ **B** I keep my prospects pretty busy...supplying information, offering suggestions, making decisions, and the like.

☐ **C** My client service is turnkey: When I'm on the case, the prospect never needs to lift a finger!

GROUP 10

☐ **A** My prospects don't usually have a lot of questions about the proposal, because there's very little in it they haven't already seen and blessed.

☐ **B** I follow the prospect's specs and requirements to a tee, so there's rarely anything in my proposal for them to question.

☐ **C** I typically get lots of questions when I present my proposal...and I'm always hoping they're ones I have good answers for!

GROUP 11

☐ **A** Sure, I encounter the usual resistance to my proposals—that's what sales is all about.

☐ **B** Once my proposal is in the prospect's hands, any resistance there may have been has already been resolved.

☐ **C** I don't get much resistance to my proposals because I present exactly what was requested.

GROUP 12

- [ ] **A** My proposals result in immediate orders far more often than those of my colleagues.
- [ ] **B** I know the prospect needs to compare my proposal with others she's received, so I allow plenty of time.
- [ ] **C** I find myself calling the prospect more often *after* I've presented the proposal than I did before.

GROUP 13

- [ ] **A** My clients get precisely what they ask for, and they're responsible for how well it performs.
- [ ] **B** If my product or service doesn't perform as promised, my clients hold me fully responsible. It comes with the territory!
- [ ] **C** I share accountability for performance with my clients; we both feel responsible to each other.

GROUP 14

- [ ] **A** I know there's a certain percentage of clients who are gonna get cold feet and cancel on me.
- [ ] **B** Perhaps I'm just lucky, but buyer's remorse is something I hardly ever encounter.
- [ ] **C** My clients rarely get cold feet because I make sure they get exactly the product or service they asked for.

GROUP 15

- [ ] **A** Conflicts can arise, but I act to resolve them early, before they can damage the relationship.
- [ ] **B** Conflict is natural in selling, because the buyer has one objective and the seller has another.
- [ ] **C** There's no need for conflict in professional selling; I make sure never to ruffle feathers.

GROUP 16

☐ **A** I think clients are generally truthful after you've known them a while, but the only way you can really build trust is over time.

☐ **B** Someone once told me that "buyers are liars." And I've seen plenty of that in my time in this business.

☐ **C** Trust isn't something I ask for, it's something I earn. I start earning it before I even meet the prospect.

GROUP 17

☐ **A** I don't like to interrogate the prospect. He'll share the information, eventually, when he thinks there is a reason for me to know.

☐ **B** I'm well-known as someone who asks a lot of questions. If I don't understand the situation, I can't help craft a solution.

☐ **C** By now, I know pretty well what questions to ask to get the information I need to present my best proposal.

GROUP 18

☐ **A** There's nothing better than "the art of the deal." A little showbiz adds drama. I love walking in with a proposal that blows the prospect away!

☐ **B** I let the prospect be the star. If anyone is up on a pedestal, it's her, not me. And that's how my proposals read too.

☐ **C** Almost everything in my proposal has already been discussed, so there is seldom any "wow factor" on presentation day. We just tie up loose ends.

GROUP 19

☐ **A** My clients don't want to hear from me unless there's an issue. They know they can count on me to handle everything.

☐ **B** I treat them more like partners than customers. It's important that we communicate a lot—before they buy and after they've bought.

☐ **C** I hate bothering a client unless absolutely necessary. A professional salesperson strives to take care of all the details. That's just good service.

GROUP 20

☐ **A** People naturally grapple with big decisions. What I've found works best with my prospects is to break big decisions down into their component parts.

☐ **B** Most people really don't like to make decisions, so I only ask them to make the minimum number of decisions necessary to get the deal done.

☐ **C** Decision-making is the client's prerogative. My job is to get as close as possible to what they asked for, but the decision is up to them.

Be sure you have placed the appropriate number next to *each* of the 60 statements. I'll provide the answer key, so you can score and analyze your responses, in Chapter 3.

ESCAPING FROM OLD HABITS

For hundreds of years, salespeople made their living by tricking or conning customers into buying things neither the sellers nor the buyers were certain they needed. Whether selling shoes, siding, or securities, sellers long peddled their wares like snake oil. This image of salespeople lives on despite decades of books, articles, seminars, and workshops about the value of being *consultative* and *customer-focused*. Like the hearty cockroach, it survives, defying a flood of evidence demonstrating the benefits of building enduring client/vendor partnerships. Why? Of course, part of the answer is that some salespeople remain clueless about the value of being truly customer-focused. But millions get it; millions really do strive to form durable partnerships and deliver strong value. So there has to be more to it.

The answer may lie in the wisdom of famed economist John Maynard Keynes, who noted, "The real difficulty in changing the course of any enterprise lies not in developing new ideas, but in escaping from the old ones." All but a few of today's salespeople, having read a recent book on sales or attended an uplifting seminar or workshop on selling, venture forth with new ideas and renewed enthusiasm about focusing on customer needs, about over-delivering on promises, about maximizing value for their customers, and about *schmearing* 'em with service...but they do so laden with old styles, old habits, and old practices. And they never realize the paradox. Their old sales cloak makes them appear to be just another salesman, just slick enough, just sleazy enough, just selfish enough, or just pre-scripted enough to come across as much less than they really are. Are you still wearing an old sales cloak? You are, if you:

Too many salespeople don't realize that what's in their heart is not what's on their sleeve.

○ Carve out enough time in each sales call to ensure you can accomplish your objectives, but fail to allocate time for the prospect to accomplish hers.

○ Ensure that your agenda is completed on every call, while not even inquiring as to the prospect's agenda or priorities.

- Ask every question that will help you sell your product or service, but none of the questions that will help him buy.

- Interpret the prospect's questions as evidence of challenge or doubt, rather than a search for information to help her buy.

- Expect the prospect to trust you, without trusting the prospect enough even to share control over the pace and direction of the sales call.

- Read resistance as an obstacle in your selling process, instead of as a significant crossroads in his buying process.

- Believe the responsibility to create a buyable proposal is entirely yours, and that prospects just want you to submit.

- *Are present for every step in the selling process, but absent for every step in the buying process.*

Too often, salespeople loaded up on customer focus and determined to dazzle their prospects with service and value still fail to produce the positive customer responses they seek. And the bigger the prospect, the more likely the failure.

EVIDENCE OF NEGLECT

You may think you're already an interactive salesperson, already paying attention to the buying process, and that you've been working this way for years, even decades. But most of you are not. Here are 14 signs you'll see if you're neglecting half your job:

1. **There is a low frequency of contact.** There aren't very many meetings, phone calls, or e-mails between you and the prospect. You had that one face-to-face, but between then and the upcoming meeting in which you expect to ask for the order,

you haven't heard from the prospect, nor has she heard from you. She has no idea what you're cooking up, and you have no notion of whether she'll find it tasty.

2. **You have unspoken assumptions and unasked questions.** You consciously decide not to question the prospect about something you know is important, so as not to stir up trouble, raise doubts, take any more time than you already have, or open a can of worms you just don't want to deal with right now. How often do you later wish you'd asked about it—because it would have eliminated trouble, rather than stirring it up?

3. **There are obvious expectation gaps.** There are little disappointments and those awkward moments when one or both of you discovers that what you were thinking or expecting was quite different from what the other was thinking or expecting. The expectation could be as simple as how long a given appointment would last, or as deal-busting as how high the price tag would be.

4. **There is tension you can cut with a knife.** The prospect distrusts you from the outset, not wanting to grant you very much time, or giving brief, largely useless answers. Or perhaps it happens later on, when he suddenly clams up and the flow of information drops to just a trickle. Sometimes it's you who doesn't trust the buyer, so you know exactly what it feels like when he doesn't trust you!

5. **You forget there's a buying process going on.** You get so wrapped up in qualifying the prospect, nailing down her needs, and crafting your proposal, that you give no time to considering the steps the prospect must go through before

she'll be able to say yes to your proposal. You carry on unaware until she says something that reveals she's way back there at step one, or maybe step one-and-a-half.

6. **The prospect loses touch with the selling process.** There's been so much going on in the prospect's world since your previous appointment that he seems to be on a different planet now. He remembers you, but he's unable to recall what you related to him last time or even what he told you...his needs, his issues, his expectations. It seems as though you have to start over.

7. **Their needs changed and you didn't know it.** It took a while to assemble your proposal, and in the meantime there has been a material change that made your proposal at least slightly off focus, if not totally off base. But your lack of interaction kept you in the dark. Weeks don't have to pass for a prospect's needs to change—it can happen overnight, perhaps the result of a meeting the prospect had with one of your competitors.

8. **She gives you endless grief about every element of your proposal.** You know she's not out to get you—at least, you hope she's not—but it certainly seems that way, because you can't get through a single piece of your plan without a tough cross-examination. You worked hard to come up with the right plan for this prospect's needs, and the thanks you get? Doubt, skepticism, and hostility.

9. **Your price is too high for the prospect even to consider.** Or there's some other element of your proposal that marks it dead-on-arrival. The prospect shows no particular interest in having you rework the plan and resubmit, and instead rises to shake your hand, says thanks, and shows you

out. You could fight your way back in, but you wonder if it's worth it.

10. **The prospect takes all your hard work for granted.** This one galls you. The prospect is dismissive of the effort you put into crafting a solution for his needs. He acts as if all you did was grab a package off the shelf, that you made no effort to tailor the plan to meet his unique needs, that nothing you did deserves even a thank-you. This kind of call makes you wonder if you should even stay in sales.

11. **You often hear the "Give me some time to think about it" response.** It sounds promising—better than a rejection!—but it's the classic indicator of handoff selling. You hear it every day, or at least every day you submit a proposal to a prospect. And it's a legitimate response, because you failed to give the prospect time to think about it earlier. People do need time to consider plans and proposals, ideas and solutions—even good ones.

12. **You make too much of an investment too early.** You go all out on behalf of a new prospect, wasting valuable time that could have been invested in a better opportunity. It might be the wrong *prospect*, because they'll never turn into a good client; the wrong *person*, and sooner or later, you'll have to start over again with the right person; or the wrong *project*, and there were bigger, more important, more urgent, or more appropriate needs for you to work toward meeting and solving.

13. **There's too much time and effort spent closing.** Your calendar and to-do list are crammed with phone calls and e-mails in which you have nothing to say, nothing to add, nothing to contribute...you

struggle to find something to say other than, "So, has the decision come down yet?" That's what life is like when you've already handed off the proposal. At that point, you're just trying to push on a string, to somehow keep the proposal moving inside the prospect's company, which is darn hard to do from the outside looking in. These calls are no fun to make, and from the reactions you hear on those occasions when you get through, these calls are no fun to receive, either.

These post-handoff phone calls are no fun to make and no fun to receive.

14. **The client is contentious after the sale.** Sometimes the hardest part is not even getting the deal done—that was hard, but not as hard putting the solution into motion, keeping the client happy, holding the deal together, maintaining profitability, and sometimes even keeping everybody out of court. Too many of your clients these days act as if you're the problem, not the solution, and often the reason is that expectations about performance, about deliverables, and about return on investment (ROI), were left vague. You were thinking one thing; they were thinking something very different.

The more of these 14 signs you see in yourself, the more likely it is you're neglecting half your job. You're paying close attention to the *selling*, but scant attention to the *buying*. And you're paying the price in lost time, lost momentum, lost opportunity, lost relationships, lost sales, lost revenues, and lost income. Nothing on that list is the fault of your prospect or client—these 14 indicators point to the fact that *you're not selling interactively*.

For a great many of you, the lack of interactivity is the one piece you're missing. You're one of the legions of motivated, well-trained salespeople who continue to suffer fist-pounding frustration and lose billions of dollars in sales every year because everything you've been told about selling is still only *half the game.* No one told you that you could or should insert yourself into the buying process—or that you could and should invite your prospect into the selling process. This is the master stroke of the salesperson's craft. This is

Everything you've been told about selling is still only half the game.

what makes buyers and sellers into true partners, interdependent players who help each other get the job done, not because they're such nice people but because it's by far the best way to get their own jobs done.

A JOURNEY, NOT A DESTINATION

I believe those old sayings, "happiness is a journey, not a destination," and "success is a journey, not a destination." I bet you do too. The best way to be happy later is to start being happy now. Small successes today put us on a path to bigger successes tomorrow. The same is true of partnership, and specifically of the interactive partnerships you want to build with your prospects and clients. Enduring client partnerships are not a distant goal to be aimed at, dreamt about, or prayed for. Interactive salespeople implement partnership *at the very outset* of every relationship, and find that most clients and prospects respond and reciprocate. For interactive sellers, partnership is the process they follow, not merely the outcome they seek. It infuses their modus operandi at every step.

The two fundamental practices at the base of interactive selling are *contracting* and *partnering*. Contracting is *the management of expectations*. It's a fancy word, but it's easy to grasp the meaning. Contracting is what's happening when:

> ❍ The dentist, a long, shiny needle in his blue-gloved hand, warns you that you'll feel "a slight pinch" before he gives you a shot of Novocain.

- You tell your friend, before you leave for the game, that you want to be home by 10 o'clock to tuck in your daughter.

- The boss at your new job tells you what the business hours are in the office and what is considered appropriate office attire.

- The menu at the Thai restaurant places a little pepper icon next to items that are spicy, and then you notice some dishes have two peppers and others have three!

Contracting happens every day in myriad unconscious and mundane ways. So it's particularly surprising how often contracting *fails to happen* between salespeople and their prospects. And it's remarkable how a process as simple as contracting can have such profound impact on your success in sales. You're about to find out how.

Partnering is *the sharing of control and responsibility.* When a truly interactive salesperson is on the case, the sharing is ratcheted way up. The partners—yes, they're feeling and acting as partners even before the first deal is done—share expectations, share agendas, share information, share enthusiasm, share resources, share goals, share energy, share limitations, share control, share decisions, and share responsibility during their *first meeting* and during *every subsequent meeting*— whether those "meetings" take place face-to-face, over the phone, or via e-mail, instant messaging, or collaborative software. Partnering is the process that makes the business relationship truly interactive, that synchronizes selling and buying to the advantage of both seller and buyer.

You may or may not be an interactive salesperson already. That answer will be revealed in the next chapter. If you are, I'll help you get even better, by adding some method to your mindset. But even if you're not, you'll soon be using contracting, partnering, and all the interactive selling practices to sell *with* your clients, not *to* them, and to close like the pros.

CLOSING THE CHAPTER

I believe these are some of the key takeaways from this chapter:

- Salespeople who may have interactivity and partnership in their heart still communicate the opposite impression by repeating so many habits learned over the years or passed down from others.

- The challenge we all face in becoming truly interactive sellers was identified clearly by economist John Maynard Keynes, when he said, "The real difficulty in changing the course of any enterprise lies not in developing new ideas, but in escaping from the old ones."

- You're neglecting half your job if you're not paying as close attention to the buying that's going on as you are to the selling that's going on.

- Consider the 14 signs you're neglecting your prospect's purchasing process as a checklist—and you would prefer not to check off any item!

- For many, lack of interactivity is the only missing piece. *Interactive selling* is the master stroke of the salesperson's craft.

- Partnership is something you practice from the outset, not a vague destination you hope someday to reach.

From where you sit, what were the takeaways in this chapter that you'll most want to remember? I'd like to know what you're thinking about as you conclude this chapter. Please e-mail me at SteveMarx@InteractiveSelling.com, and be sure to put "Chapter 2" in the subject line.

CHAPTER THREE
Two Losers and Two Winners

Look across the prospect's desk. She wants to buy. If she didn't, you would never have gotten the appointment. And the vast majority of buyers welcome a little help with their buying decision, especially if it's not a purchase they've made repeatedly in the past, if their needs are a bit different this time, or if conditions in the market have changed. So it's especially ironic that so many salespeople focus so exclusively on selling, when the opportunity to help the buyer buy is quite literally staring them in the face! But most sellers remain resolutely focused on their own sales performance, their own sales pipeline, and their own sales goals, continuing to see prospective customers as nothing more than elusive prizes to be charmed, cajoled, and eventually captured.

That's not what the pros see when they look across the desk.

You can jack up the odds in your favor by realizing that your prospects are not line-items on a sales projection page, but buyers with a job to do. They fully expect to devote time, energy, information, ideas, evaluations, and judgments to the buying process. They will invest considerable effort in the hope of making a wise decision. They want your help. Indeed, that's why you're sitting across their desk. Some are accustomed to folding their arms and just listening, or dutifully responding to the seller's predetermined questions, but that's only because most of the salespeople who call on them ask no more of them. In fact, they often allow no more. Those salespeople walk in with their own agenda, complete that agenda, and walk out.

The best prospects—those with the most successful businesses, the biggest budgets, and the greatest potential to be your client-partner for years and years—aren't hooking up with salespeople who sell, sell, sell, and scoot. Would you like to know what's going through their head, while you're so focused on your sales process, your sales questions, and your sales spiel? Here are the kinds of things I've heard them say over the years about the typical noninteractive sales process:

> ○ *That salesman must have been to a seminar recently or something. I felt as though he was following some kind of step-by-step strategy and I was just a pawn. I don't know about you, but I don't buy that way.*

> ○ *For me, it's all about making a high-quality decision. That's what my boss expects; it's what she pays me to do. I don't care whose ideas lead us to that best decision, but I can tell you from experience that rarely does the salesperson have all the ideas we need. It takes both of us, and often a*

bunch of people from both his organization and ours to get it right. I rarely get that opportunity.

○ I asked her a lot of questions—I usually do!—but she had almost no questions for me. It's as if she's waiting for me to decide so she can write up the order. But I've never bought a system like this. I need some guidance.

○ Inevitably, it takes us time to review and evaluate proposals, even the ones we think we like. Any good proposal has a lot of detail, a lot of moving parts, and a lot to think about, and sometimes compare. Our work begins when that proposal arrives.

○ I don't like surprises. Don't like 'em from my boss, from my people, or from salespeople who call on me. I like to know what's happening and where we're heading. Salespeople who throw me a curve get tossed from the game.

○ The salesman asked a lot of questions, I'll give him that. I answered every single one to the best of my ability, but when he returned with the proposal, it sure didn't seem like he had grasped our real needs.

○ This proposal is confusing and hard to follow. Frankly, it's a little overwhelming; a lot to absorb all at once.

○ That sales rep was willing to sell me anything in his warehouse! Whenever I inquired about a different material or a different color, he smiled and said he could do that. I felt as though I was totally on my own to figure out the best way to go.

○ Most salespeople we see want to know all about our budget for this line-item, but they want to hold back any information about pricing or cost.

I'm not walking into that trap. I'm not just gonna share my number with the guy, because I've seen too many times when the proposal comes back right around that number. If we're talking numbers along the way, and we should be, it's gotta be his numbers and ours.

○ *I'll tell ya, I really liked the basic approach she took with that solution, but she really should have run it all by me much earlier. With what I know, I could have improved her proposed plan about 500 percent. Now what? Do I send it back for her to rework it, or do I just go with the Acme proposal that doesn't need that kind of redo?*

○ *Vendors are a dime a dozen. We're cutting way back on the number of vendors we do business with. If they're not good partners, good collaborators, willing to work closely with us, we're gonna find someone else.*

○ *Where on Earth did this plan come from? We only spoke once, and then this salesperson took the whole thing in the wrong direction. He just wasted my time.*

The scenario is different when there's an *interactive salesperson* across the desk. The interactive seller won't let the prospect be disengaged—or take over the call, for that matter. He won't grow his proposal in the dark, out of sight and out of reach of his prospect. He won't throw curves or ask his prospect to buy something she hasn't already seen, understood, and smiled about. He won't ignore the buying process or leave it to begin only after he's handed off his proposal. The interactive seller's approach is designed around *activating* the prospect, making her an equal participant in the selling, and himself an equal participant in the buying. He

The sooner the buying begins, the better it is for both.

understands that her job is to buy, and the sooner the buying begins the better it is for both of them.

Your prospects are more than willing to do some work, sometimes a lot of work, to make sure they get the right proposal and to ensure that they are investing their money wisely. They will follow your lead: If you ignore their buying process, they'll just wait until you've submitted before rolling up their sleeves and considering your proposal. But if you work with them from the outset, they'll work with you. If you help them jump-start the buying process, you'll stay involved in it—because you've placed the relationship on an interactive path, one focused as much on buying as on selling.

It's not something you claim— it's something you do

There's a name for that interactive path. It's called *partnering*. It's how the pros close. Partnering is how the world's best sales professionals steer any deal that's large, complex, creative, new, or competitive toward a successful conclusion. For the pros, partnership is not a vague destination they hope someday to reach with a few of their clients, but rather, *a way of doing business.* Those who get it—who use interactive selling and behave as partners from their first words—create more highly satisfied clients, longer-lasting relationships, and higher revenues.

Partnership is an overused and abused buzzword—but remains an underused practice.

Ironically, the more salespeople talk about partnering and partnerships, the less likely it is they are actually doing it. As a popular term in business culture, "partnership" is overdone. As a true practice, it's rare. Interactive selling is not about using the word *partner* or the word *partnership*. It's about *being* a partner.

Ordinary salespeople—those who fail to reach their goals consistently—see partnership as a distant dream, a hoped-for outcome worthy of serious contemplation only after many orders and reorders, only after a series of projects, assignments, or deals. They don't see themselves as a partner, so they don't act as a partner would, and neither do their prospects and most of their clients.

Successful salespeople—the crème de la crème who beat their numbers month in and month out and win the big awards—see partnership as something they do every day with every prospect and every client, built on mutual respect, mutual effort, and mutual benefit. These interactive salespeople know that partnership starts from the first contact with the prospect and never ends. For them, partnership is not a long-term goal, but rather a process—a set of behaviors—that is active and vibrant during all phases of the sales process and beyond.

Partnering—the sharing of control and accountability—is a decision the salesperson makes, and it's one of the smartest decisions any salesperson will ever make. As a buzzword, it's overused. As a practice, it can't be used enough.

BULLDOZER, GOFER, OR PARTNER— TWO LOSERS AND A WINNER

The Interactive Partner is the rare exception in today's sales force. Most salespeople are either too pushy or too passive in their work with prospects, and some remain so even with some long-standing clients. Both are easy behaviors to fall into because most of us naturally emulate the way we see others act. We've been observing pushy sellers and passive sellers our entire life, so the pattern persists, without much planning or insight, as each of us leans toward either passiveness or pushiness. Both are troubling because they leave one party out of the process. Neither one can be interactive selling.

Sales Relationship Matrix

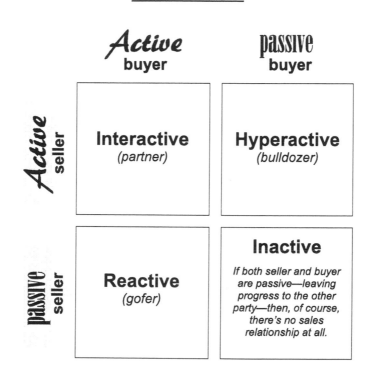

Active buyer   **passive** buyer

Active seller

Interactive
(partner)

Hyperactive
(bulldozer)

passive seller

Reactive
(gofer)

Inactive

If both seller and buyer are passive—leaving progress to the other party—then, of course, there's no sales relationship at all.

Every sales relationship can be characterized by who is playing an *active role* and who—if anyone—is playing a *passive role*. The Sales Relationship Matrix shown here charts the three *sales relationship types*. You may have client relationships that fall into all three types—many salespeople do. But most of the thousands of sellers I've met over the years find that the bulk of their client relationships fall into one of the three basic sales relationship types. Here's a thumbnail description of each:

HYPERACTIVE SALESPERSON—
THE BULLDOZER

Bill is a bulldozer. He's a classic *hyperactive* seller, a guy who *owns* the process right up until the handoff. Bill takes sole control and makes all the decisions—about what his prospect needs and how to fill that need. He's active every minute; his prospect is passive. It's not that he's heavy-handed or unpleasant in any way—in fact, Bill is immensely charming and plenty of fun to be around—but he functions as a bulldozer, as a very nice know-it-all. Perhaps it's because he really believes he knows better than does his prospect, or because he's seen situations such as this before and always suggests the same approach or the same solution, or just because Bill's in a hurry and believes the prospect too is in a hurry, and so he "cuts to the chase."

Taken to the extreme, the hyperactive salesperson is the door-to-door vacuum-cleaner salesman of days long past who's through your front door before you know it, and who doesn't just *determine* the problem but actually *creates* it by dumping a load of manure on your beige living-room carpet. But fear not! The bulldozer has the solution to your problem at his fingertips: It's his latest vacuum-cleaner model, of course, and it will suck up that stinking mess (and any small pets you may have walking around) before you can dial 911.

Unfortunately, the hyperactive sales type didn't die with the old-fashioned hucksters and con artists who made it notorious. He—or she, because Bettys can be just as guilty of bulldozing as some Bills are—is still the most common kind of seller out there, aided and abetted by all those books (and sales managers) telling you to "stay in control." The hyperactive bulldozer category includes some sellers who appear quite sophisticated in their methods. Any seller whose paradigm and policy is always to stay in firm control of the sales process is looking at a bulldozer every time she peers into a mirror. And any seller who fails to use interactive selling consistently and creatively is acting like a bulldozer, even if high-pressure tactics are the farthest thing from his mind.

The unfortunate truth is that *most* salespeople are hyperactive *most* of the time. And most of the sales training, coaching, and supervision we're subjected to is out to make bulldozers of us all.

REACTIVE SALESPERSON—THE GOFER

Gail is everything Bill isn't. She's a perfect example of a *reactive* seller, the direct opposite of the hyperactive. Gail is every bit as affable and friendly as Bill is, so it takes a moment to recognize the huge difference in the way each of them approaches the sale. She tends to be passive, deferring to her prospect to play the active role. Gail lets the prospect make all the decisions, be they small or large, and we nickname this sales type the gofer, because she's quite content simply to carry out the client's wishes—go fer this, go fer that, go fer whatever the prospect or client wants, whether it's smart or not. Ever eager to please, our gofer Gail yields control, responding not with ideas, suggestions, or alternative approaches, but with a smile, a lunch, and a bid.

Yes, Gail is more order-taker than salesperson—and she crosses her fingers that the prospect will place an order. By being accommodating to a fault, Gail is cheating herself, her employer, and even her client out of potential profits. She leaves the better solutions for her competitor to suggest, she leaves the larger orders on the table, and she leaves the longer-term partnerships for other salespeople.

Some buyers believe they have it all figured out in advance, and don't even call for a salesperson until they need a gofer...to execute their predetermined solution or simply to find the lowest bidder. This scenario is especially common when dealing with purchasing agents, but we all encounter such "bulldozer buyers" from time to time. Occasionally, the expedient choice is to be the gofer he wants you to be, but often you'll find that you can form an interactive relationship based on certain capabilities you bring to the table. The reactive gofer is often—but not always—a bit more laid-back than other salespeople, and especially tends to be less intense than the hyperactive bulldozer. But in this sales type, as with the others, we find plenty of Georges, not just Gails.

INTERACTIVE SALESPERSON— THE PARTNER

Pat is a Pro! Pat is the quintessential interactive salesperson, the partner who believes control and accountability should be shared between the buyer and the seller...not only because it's the right thing to do, but because it's the path that leads to dramatically greater success. Pat too is friendly and engaging, not unlike Bill and Gail, but Pat's process is totally different from theirs. When Pat's on the case, everyone is active. Pat engages the prospect on a business level as well as a social level, integrating the selling and buying processes artfully and seamlessly. Clients work side by side with Pat to identify the issues, nail down the needs, define the details, and work their way toward win-win.

Partners such as Pat use the principles and practices of interactive selling to ensure that both they and their clients attack the challenge together, rather than attacking each other. Together, they roll up their sleeves and get their hands dirty, knowing that the best solutions emerge when the buyer and seller both are actively involved. They're partners right now in creating the proposal, not just later on, when the time comes to implement it. An enduring customer/vendor partnership is not, for them, a matter of luck or happenstance, but of intent. It is the natural outcome of having conducted themselves as partners throughout the relationship, beginning even before the first contact.

Bulldozers and gofers are the *long-term losers* in the world of sales. They may enjoy the occasional good year, but they never consistently rank near the top—in their company's rankings or their client's. The sales pros who do the biggest deals, who have the strongest client satisfaction and highest retention rates, who outperform their peers and soar past their goals, who are *wide-margin winners*—they're partners!

It takes no more talent to be interactive than it does to be hyperactive or reactive.

Learning to be an interactive partner is within the reach of every bulldozer Bill and gofer Gail who carries an account list. It takes no more talent to be interactive than it does to be hyperactive or reactive—just the desire to learn how to close like the pros and the willingness to implement a few new practices. In fact, Pat admits to having been a bit of a bulldozer before learning why and how to be an interactive seller. If Pat can do it, you can do it.

WHICH SALES TYPE ARE YOU?

Now you're *really* wondering how you scored on the self-assessment survey you completed near the beginning of Chapter 2. If you skipped past it, you might want to jet back there now and complete it. Or perhaps you chose to complete the survey online at *www.InteractiveSelling.com*. If so, the results are already waiting for you in your e-mail inbox (if you don't see the e-mail from us in your inbox, please check your junk mail folder, as it may have landed there).

Assuming you filled in your numbers for all 60 items, it's time to transfer those numbers onto the scoring key shown here— and learn where you placed yourself in the Sales Relationship Matrix: hyperactive bulldozer, reactive gofer, or interactive partner.

Transfer your numbers carefully. It's easy to get confused. For each group of statements, you want to place your number on this scoring key next to the same letter it's next to on the instrument in Chapter 2. Note that the letters move around on the scoring key; they appear in different columns for each group of statements. Be very careful to place the correct number next to each letter. Then add up the figures in each column. (By the way, your three final scores at the bottom of the key should total 120; if they don't, you have a mistake somewhere.)

SCORING KEY

GROUP 1	☐ B	☐ A	☐ C
GROUP 2	☐ A	☐ B	☐ C
GROUP 3	☐ C	☐ B	☐ A
GROUP 4	☐ A	☐ C	☐ B
GROUP 5	☐ B	☐ A	☐ C
GROUP 6	☐ C	☐ B	☐ A
GROUP 7	☐ C	☐ A	☐ B
GROUP 8	☐ A	☐ B	☐ C

GROUP 9	☐	C	☐	A	☐	B
GROUP 10	☐	C	☐	B	☐	A
GROUP 11	☐	A	☐	C	☐	B
GROUP 12	☐	C	☐	B	☐	A
GROUP 13	☐	B	☐	A	☐	C
GROUP 14	☐	A	☐	C	☐	B
GROUP 15	☐	B	☐	C	☐	A
GROUP 16	☐	B	☐	A	☐	C
GROUP 17	☐	C	☐	A	☐	B
GROUP 18	☐	A	☐	B	☐	C
GROUP 19	☐	A	☐	C	☐	B
GROUP 20	☐	B	☐	C	☐	A
TOTALS	☐		☐		☐	
	H		**R**		**I**	

You should now have three scores at the bottom of the page:

H is your Hyperactive score.

R is your Reactive score.

I is your Interactive score.

Your highest score identifies the type of sales relationship you have with the majority of your clients and prospects. It's your "home base," your natural selling approach today. Think of your second highest score, especially if it's within 10 points of your highest, as your *secondary* sales relationship type.

Did you score as a bulldozer, a gofer, or a partner? No doubt you want to say partner, but I'll bet only 10 percent of you would actually profile that way if you answered each question carefully and honestly. In fact, my experience tells me that around 60 percent of America's sales force are hyperactive bulldozers, and another 30 percent are reactive gofers.

Now look at your Interactive score.

◯ If you answered every item honestly and sincerely, and your Interactive score is 54 or higher, congratulations! You're already an interactive salesperson, already a partner. Keep turning the pages here, because I'll put new tools and practices in your hands that will multiply your effectiveness.

◯ If your Interactive score is less than 54, but is the highest of your three scores, then you have an inclination to be Interactive, a good foundation to build upon. You too will find the tools of interactive selling enormously helpful in moving your performance to a higher level.

◯ If your leading score points toward a hyperactive or reactive sales process, or if *all* your scores fell into the 35–45 range (no strong leaning toward any of the three relationship types), rest assured, *interactive selling* is a system you can learn—and profit from.

Regardless of where on the Sales Relationship Matrix you profiled, consider the limitations inherent in any self-assessment. A few folks have extraordinary self-awareness;

they can describe accurately and faithfully just how they have behaved in a variety of scenarios and what their impact on other people has been. Others are very open to feedback from family, friends, associates, and clients, and by using this feedback they have grown to have a good understanding of themselves and how they interact with others. But there are still plenty of people— not just salespeople, but everyone—whose self-perceptions are significantly different from what others would say about them. In the weeks ahead, observe yourself more closely and look for evidence that you might be hyperactive or reactive, or, I hope, interactive!

Interactive sellers produce win-win outcomes, the foundation for continuing business.

Two losers and two winners?

You've now learned about the three basic sales relationship types—the two losers, the bulldozer and the gofer; and about the one winner, the partner. So what's with the title of this chapter? Why is it named Two Losers and Two Winners?

Many readers have probably figured it out already. Yes, the interactive seller is surely a winner. But she's not the only winner. Her client has become her *interactive partner* and he is just as big a winner. He helps her sell as she helps him buy. She sells more products, services, systems, and solutions, and they have more value because they represent a superior way to meet her clients' needs. Her clients are more likely to return, renew, and reorder, and less likely to haggle over price. The interactive partner wins big, but not at the expense of her client. She wins by helping her client win!

CLOSING THE CHAPTER

I believe these are some of the key takeaways from this chapter:

- Your prospects want to buy. If they didn't, you wouldn't be sitting in front of them.
- Prospects welcome true help. When you offer it, you'll encounter no resistance.
- Prospects want a good proposal, one that comes as close as possible to meeting their needs. They jump at the chance to help make the proposal buyable.
- Partnership is something you do...not something you claim, and not a buzzword you toss into the conversation now and then.
- Every sales relationship can be categorized by who is active and who is passive. In both the *hyperactive* and *reactive* types, one party is passive. Only the *interactive* type has two fully active partners.
- It takes no more talent to be *interactive* than it does to be hyperactive or reactive—just the desire to learn how to close like the pros and the willingness to implement a few new practices.

As you conclude this chapter, are there any points or passages you underlined or highlighted? What are the big takeaways from your point of view? Remember, you can always e-mail me at SteveMarx@InteractiveSelling.com. If you're writing now, as you conclude Chapter 3, then place "Chapter 3" in the subject line of your message.

CHAPTER FOUR

Don't Fall Into Expectation Gaps (and Gulches)

IF YOUR PRODUCT INSTALLATION OR PROCESS MODIFICATION results in a 15 percent increase in operating efficiency for your customer, is that a good outcome? The answer is yes, if the customer was expecting only a 10 percent improvement. But the answer could also be no, if the customer's expectation was to see an improvement of 25 percent or more. The actual outcome, the 15 percent improvement, has no significance until we factor in the client's expectations. One way, you're a hero; the other way, you're a goat.

I'm probably not the first person to tell you how essential it is to know the client's expectations about how your product or your solution will deliver the functionality, the benefits, and the ROI he's seeking. But you may not know that your prospect has a litany of little expectations as well—about mundane things—and if you're not fully aware of them, they can derail your sale. Indeed, if you can't meet all the small expectations along the path to the sale, you'll never have the chance to know if you could meet that prospect's *big* expectations. You'll never know if he was looking for a 10 percent improvement or a 25 percent improvement, if he has three jobs to fill or 300, if the design specs call for high-tensile strength or not. You may never get there, if you fall into an expectation gap along the way.

Think back on all the appointments that didn't go as you had hoped and planned, the calls in which you and the prospect couldn't get on the same wavelength, the first-time meetings that turned out to be last-time meetings as well. More sales are lost early on, stillborn before the first call or shortly thereafter, because the salesperson failed to discover, disclose, or manage expectations—*little ones!* It's happened to you countless times. You thought you'd have an hour with the prospect, but she thought you would be in and out in 10 minutes (and unfortunately, you were!). You thought you'd devote the call to learning more about the prospect's needs, but he was expecting a pitch about your new product line—the one in the magazine ad—and was in no mood to answer your probing questions. You thought you'd be meeting with one guy, but the secretary ushered you into a conference room with 14 executives, and because you had brought only two copies of your leave-behind materials, you looked generally inept and unprepared.

Most sales are stillborn— because the seller failed to manage the little expectations.

Sometimes, as in these examples, it's painfully obvious that your expectation and the prospect's were not quite aligned. There's always the chance to recover, to struggle out of an expectation gulch you may have fallen into, and I'm sure you can recall occasions when you've done just that. What's scary is to ponder all the times when you had no notion that the prospect was expecting yin and you were delivering yang. Often, the only feedback we ever get is silence—calls not returned, e-mails not answered.

The prospect is under no obligation to tell you that she's confused or disappointed, that her expectations are not being met at this moment. You often don't disclose that, either! You pride yourself on being flexible and adroit, so rather than inform the prospect that your agenda differs from hers, you suck it up, you soldier on, and you make the best of it. It happens in your personal life too. You thought the gang was going to see the latest 3-D thriller at the multiplex, so you brought your 3-D glasses…but the guys had bowed to pressure from the ladies and decided to catch the chick flick instead. You suffered in silence, and kept those old 3-D glasses out of sight! Then there was the time your best friend from college was in town and told you he'd see you at 7 p.m. for dinner. You prepared your famous duck l'orange. He made reservations downtown. When he arrived at your front door and told you to grab your coat because the reservation was at 7:15, you smiled and never mentioned the duck.

When we stumble into little expectation gaps with our friends, we nearly always recover. We cut them some slack, and they do the same for us. We vow—or make a mental note—to be a bit more explicit next time. In business, that rarely happens. You might be more than willing to overlook almost any curve a prospect may toss at you, but you're having a lucky day when the prospect forgives you for disappointing or confusing him. Most of the time, he handles it quietly, with a pocket veto. You'll never see him again.

Your friends will cut you some slack; your prospects will just give you a pocket veto.

IT'S NOT ENOUGH THAT *you* KNOW WHERE YOU'RE GOING

What's fascinating is that, while in our personal lives we make that mental note to be more explicit next time to align our expectations more clearly, very few salespeople take that same common sense into their job. Most salespeople approach a new prospect with some sort of plan in mind—a method they have learned, a system they have perfected, perhaps a series of steps or phases. The seller's plan is set. He knows where he's going. The only trouble is:

- The prospect doesn't know where the seller is going.

- The seller doesn't know what the prospect would think or how the prospect would feel about where they're going, if she only knew.

- The salesperson is clueless about what direction the prospect herself might like to take.

Does all this make a difference? When you and your prospect are on a different wavelength about the little things—such as what's going to take place next time you meet—it's nearly impossible to get together on the big things. That's *not* because you'll be unable or unwilling to discuss the big expectations—the performance, utility, and value of your proposed solution, for example—but simply because you won't get that far! When you can't connect on the little things, the relationship sours, your credibility suffers, your reliability is called into question, and the foundation of trust it takes to do business never develops.

The sooner the buying begins, the better it is for both.

It's amazing how often salespeople don't even understand how or why they got the appointment! And yet, they plow ahead (or plod ahead), following a script or a sequence known only to themselves and approved only by themselves. That's no way to be a partner. It's not even a good way to get an order.

CHRIS ISN'T CONTRACTING

When Chris showed up for her 2:30 p.m. appointment with Lee Jones, she was a bit surprised by his attire. Lee greeted her at the door wearing golfing clothes.

"How much time do you need?" Lee asked. "I need to leave for a golf outing in 15 minutes."

Is it good or bad that the client in this example has 15 minutes to spend with the salesperson? Well, it's good if Chris only expected to get five minutes, but it's bad if she expected an hour.

Our story might have continued this way:

Chris smiled and shook her head. "I just wanted to drop off our most recent brochure," she said. "We can talk about it in a few days, after you've had a chance to review the latest additions to our product line. I'll call you Tuesday afternoon."

The outcome in this case was comfortable for both the client and the salesperson. Chris expected simply to drop off the brochure, and Lee was counting on her to be in and out in a flash.

But what if the meeting had gone this way:

Chris bit back her disappointment. She had planned a one-hour presentation for Lee, and had hoped to interest him in a special opportunity that was due to expire in a few days. Now it seemed clear that she wouldn't be able to use the presentation she'd prepared—unless she could find a way to make it work right now. She saw Lee glance at his watch.

"Mr. Jones," Chris began, trying not to whine, "I really need an hour of your time. Can I tag along? I promise it will be worth your while."

Annoyance flashed across Lee's face. "I guess you can ride along with me to the golf course, but your time is up the moment we get to the clubhouse. I've got a tee time with a very important customer. Then he and I have a lengthy business agenda over dinner."

Give Chris some points for being creative, for trying to find a compromise quickly. But now she's put herself into a tough environment, trying to pitch to a prospect while's he's picking his way through traffic and thinking about his business-critical tee-time. Better than nothing? Doubtful. Preventable? Probably. Chris should have contracted expectations with Lee as carefully as Lee had obviously contracted expectations with his very important client. Compared to Lee's carefully crafted arrangements, Chris' sales call was a failure.

ARRANGE, DON'T HOPE

In the first scenario, Chris got lucky: she needed less than 15 minutes of the client's time. But in the second scenario, both Chris and the client were unhappy—Chris because she'd spent a great deal of time preparing a presentation she now couldn't deliver or had to deliver under adverse circumstances without all the visuals she had prepared, and Lee because he was being asked to focus on and devote attention to something on which he hadn't planned. Chris' credibility, the foundation of trust in a business relationship, is crumbling.

Expectations are powerful—so powerful, in fact, that they can make or break a meeting. And it's not only expectations about how long a meeting will take that are important. Other expectations influence the outcome as well, such as:

○ The purpose of the meeting.

○ Who is going to be in attendance.

○ Topics on—and off—the agenda.

○ The desired result(s) of the meeting.

○ Others that depend on the specific circumstances.

Think about your own experience. How often has it become obvious—early in a meeting or even well into it—that your notion of what the meeting was about and the prospect's notion were rather different? If it's only your first or second meeting, you'll see evidence such as:

○ Your prospect suddenly looks confused or uncomfortable, and acts in awkward or puzzling ways.

○ Your prospect clams up when the direction you take or the questions you ask seem off-topic to her, or when they strike her as unnecessarily probing or deep.

○ Your prospect takes the meeting in a direction you were not prepared for.

If you're much further into the sales process, or perhaps if this prospect is already a client of yours, the evidence of expectations not addressed and aligned includes things such as:

○ The client is shocked, or really thrown off, by the cost of your proposed project or solution.

○ Either he or you—or more likely both of you—wonder just where you stand with each other now.

○ You're forced to devote time and effort to fix something that went wrong, such as a relationship, proposal, or implementation.

Think about the most recent in-person sales call you made, probably earlier today:

○ Did you have a clear picture of the client's expectations regarding agenda, process, and outcome? Or did you assume?

○ Had you thought clearly about your own expectations? And did it occur to you not to leave them
unsaid?

○ Did you and the client take the time to share your
expectations *with each other*—beyond just speci-
fying the date, time, and location of the meeting?
Or were you just hoping it would all work out?

When expectations are left unstated and unaligned, the
course and outcome of the meeting—and indeed, the entire
relationship—is left to chance.

Now think about your next appointment, the one scheduled for tomorrow morning:

○ Do you know your expectations for the meeting?

○ Have you taken the time to communicate them?

○ Have you asked your prospect or client what her
expectations are?

○ Are your expectations and hers *consistent* with
each other, and will they make for a successful
appointment?

If you find yourself answering no to many of these questions, you have a lot of company. Most of us assume (incor-
rectly) that we know what our clients want and expect from
their time with us, not to mention their *relationships* with us.
But the ugly truth is *we don't know*. And we aren't going to
know unless we ask.

HOW TO AVOID THE DITCH

Everyone has expectations, conscious and unconscious,
stated and unstated, aligned, unaligned, or misaligned. Every
prospect, every client, every seller, every buyer, every reader—
every person. Expectations need to be addressed and aligned,
or we fall into a gulch, or drive into a ditch. That's why the

pros, the interactive sellers who are the envy of their less-successful colleagues, contract expectations. They contract consciously and constantly. *Contracting* is a fancy word for a simple process, and it will revolutionize your results. Contracting is *managing expectations*, upfront—not to get yourself out of the ditch, but to avoid it altogether.

Expectations need to be addressed and aligned.

Contracting is largely ignored by most salespeople—all the hyperactive and reactive types—and yet, there's a simple and intuitive level of contracting that no one ever ignores. It's so intuitive, in fact, that you do it several times a day without giving it a second thought:

> ○ You're contracting when you arrange to meet your kids right next to the equipment building at the soccer field at 4:45 p.m.

> ○ You're contracting when you decide with a friend to catch the early movie and then enjoy a late supper at The Bistro.

> ○ You're contracting when you agree to see your accountant tomorrow morning at 9 a.m. in Conference Room A on the 22nd floor.

You're contracting with your clients and prospects every time you set an appointment for a specific date, time, and place. No meeting has ever taken place without at least that much contracting having first been done.

But there are more expectations to be managed than simply time and place. You and your prospect are not truly contracting unless you are addressing and aligning *all* of the expectations each of you has about your upcoming meeting. Each expectation not surfaced and dealt with could open up a gap or a gulch.

Both of you have a lot of expectations, including some you may never have thought about before—at least not consciously. Here are some that impact your early-stage meetings and dealings:

Ground rules. They're not "rules," per se. These mutually agreed-upon conditions govern the *process* of the meeting, so that, for example, both buyer and seller set aside the same amount of time, bring the appropriate information or resources, and attend either alone or with the agreed-upon people from each company.

Clear paths and genuine agendas. Why have you proposed a meeting? Why has the prospect agreed to meet with you? What topics are on the table? How far does each of you hope to get in the upcoming meeting? This is all about how the appointment will feel and how it will flow. Then, when you get together, you're both on the same page. No awkward moments, no surprises, no disappointments.

As detailed in Chapter 5, you may not be able to get all your expectations for that meeting out into the open, but don't be too quick to settle for just time and place. Any important expectation of yours or theirs that isn't shared and dealt with is similar to a heap of boulders piled on the tracks just around the next bend, waiting to derail your sale.

If you survive the first face-to-face meeting or two, mutual trust and comfort begin to develop. You might think, for your subsequent meetings, the list of expectations to be managed would start to shrink. On the contrary, it *expands*. Ground rules keep evolving, as do paths and agendas. For the interactive seller, these are all opportunities to partner, to share control and accountability, and to begin closing. Closing? Of course! Among the many decisions a prospect must make before he signs on your dotted line is whether he can trust you, can rely on you, can sleep at night after he says yes. At this point in your relationship, you might already have that piece of the deal "closed."

As time goes on, the list of expectations to manage doesn't shrink— it expands.

There's plenty more for the interactive seller to contract, to close, before the sale is finally confirmed. She accurately sees each of these partnering opportunities as "mini-closes," as steps toward the sale, and steps the prospect takes toward the purchase. Buying and selling become integrated into a single, seamless process with these interactive selling practices:

Homework assignments. Simply arranging the time and place to meet next is an insufficient way to end a meeting. To move the relationship and the sale forward, you need to contract, to spell out, *who* is going to do *what* between now and the next meeting. Both partners, buyer *and* seller, need to leave with an assignment that the other party expects them to complete before the next meeting. You'll find *homework assignments* probed in detail in Chapter 8.

Half-baked ideas. Sharing ideas and possible solutions while they're still vague concepts or sketchy notions is so much more powerful and partner-esque than presenting done deals and fait accompli. It doesn't get much more interactive than this. The prospect, seeing or hearing your *half-baked ideas,* has the opportunity to reject the ones that don't feel right or just can't work, focus on the ones that do, and then finish "baking" an idea or two in his own mental oven. More about the magic of *underselling* in Chapter 9.

Trial Balloons. It's important to contract every significant element of the plan or solution that's starting to take shape well before that day you're looking for a signature. The price and terms of the solution you're assembling with the prospect is just one such element on which your expectations need to be aligned. If you want to score a yes, it's important to *know every no*, which is why you'll want to read about how the pros *trial balloon everything* in Chapter 10.

Progress Reports. Interactive selling requires checking in with your prospect on a regular basis to make sure she's continuing to think along the same lines you are. If you're selling a complex solution, or one that involves a number of decision-influencers or a long selling cycle, you will benefit tremendously from issuing periodic, written *progress reports.* Firmer than half-baked ideas, these pre-proposals are intended to help lock down—close!—certain concepts, elements, and details, allowing the partners to focus on the remaining open issues. Expect more about *progress reports* in Chapter 11.

No-Surprise Proposal. It's so much easier to sell a proposal when the prospect has already "bought" every page in it. It's how the pros close. And it's just the opposite of how the bulldozers and gofers of this world do it. Take the drama—and the doubt—out of your proposals by making them simply a written specification of what everybody has already agreed to. Ordinary salespeople pop the proposal as early as possible and wait for the close; interactive sellers start mini-closing way up front and hold delivery of the written proposal until the yes is ready. The *no-surprise proposal* is detailed in Chapter 11.

Critical Path. The *critical path* carries the contracting process through the confirmation of the order and right into the implementation phase of the partnership. It's a one-page document that serves as the last page of your formal proposal; it reviews the steps you and your client-partner took to develop the solution together, and then goes on to detail each of the steps that must be taken to implement the plan and achieve the desired results. You'll learn how to build a critical path that works in Chapter 11.

Some of these interactive selling practices may seem familiar to you; others may appear novel, puzzling, or even downright strange. They're all designed to close expectation gaps and keep you out of deep gulches. Every one of them is easy to do. As soon as you begin blending them into your daily sales life, you'll begin to *close like the pros!*

CLOSING THE CHAPTER

I believe these are some of the key takeaways from this chapter:

- More sales are lost early on, stillborn before the first call or shortly thereafter, because the salesperson failed to discover, disclose, or manage expectations—*little ones!*

- Misaligned expectations are often forgiven among friends, but rarely forgiven or forgotten between salesperson and prospect.

- When you and your prospect are on a different wavelength about the little things—such as what's going to take place next time you meet—it's nearly impossible to get together on the big things.

- Expectations are so powerful they can make or break a meeting, a relationship, and a business deal.

- Contracting is the process of addressing and aligning expectations, and while it's simple and easy, it remains largely ignored by most salespeople.

- Contracting is necessary, not just at the start of the selling process, but at every step along the way.

Those are the big takeaways—from my point of view. But I wonder what it looks like to you. Which concepts here made the biggest impression on you? Tell me about it. E-mail me at SteveMarx@InteractiveSelling.com, and remember to put "Chapter 4" in your subject line.

CHAPTER FIVE

REPLACE RELATIONSHIP TENSION WITH TASK TENSION

CONVENTIONAL WISDOM SAYS TENSION IN A BUSINESS setting is a bad omen, and little progress will be made until it's removed. That's true in the case of unhealthy *relationship tension*, but not its healthy counterpart, *task tension*. These two types of tension are akin to the two types of cholesterol—what doctors call bad cholesterol and good cholesterol—*one needs to be lowered and the other one raised.*

Just as we can't have too much good cholesterol coursing through our arteries, there's no such thing as too much task tension. Task tension is that nearly intoxicating intensity, power, and direction you feel when you and your prospect are fully focused and moving forward. You're zeroed in on the issues, the creative juices are pumping, and ideas and possibilities are popping from all corners of the room—you are "in the flow." You've probably had some appointments that went this way, so you know just how cool it is when healthy task tension takes over. It's when buyer and seller are both so actively engaged in identifying the problem or opportunity and creating the solution that they lose all track of time and don't even notice that everyone else has gone to lunch!

Task tension is that intoxicating intensity, power, and direction you sometimes feel when you and your prospect are truly collaborating.

When task tension is high, when everyone has rolled up their sleeves and are working as peers in a spirit of cooperation and common cause, you're watching *interactive selling* in action! The client is helping the salesperson perfect the proposal, and the seller is helping the client clarify his issues and lock down the pieces and parts of the solution, one piece and one part at a time. It's time well spent for both partners, and *partners* they truly are. Because you've been in a few meetings similar to that, and a handful of enduring business relationships of that sort, you know how precious they are.

And you also know how rare they are. But reaching the truly interactive sales relationship isn't a matter of luck, it's a matter of skill. The fundamental skills are *contracting* (the management of expectations) and *partnering* (the sharing of control and accountability). Before we can turn up the task tension, we have to deal with the relationship tension.

Relationship tension is the bad cholesterol that blocks your sales arteries, keeping you "out of the flow." Relationship tension remains stubbornly persistent, obstructing task tension, so long as key relationship questions remain unanswered. Both you and your prospect have questions, concerns, anxieties, and doubts—and they don't benefit from benign neglect; they don't naturally fade away if you ignore them. He'll rarely give voice to them, but here are some of the questions and concerns your prospect has about you:

○ Does this person know what she's talking about?

○ Does she care about me and my business?

○ Does she have a hidden agenda?

○ What's her track record?

○ What sort of training or certification does she have?

○ How long has she had the job?

○ Does she know more than I do about what she's selling?

○ Will she dress and act in a professional manner?

○ Can she be trusted?

○ What will she do with the information I share with her?

○ Will she care enough to take account of my unique issues and constraints?

○ Will she really tailor her proposal?

○ Will she deliver on promises?

○ Will she stay beyond her welcome?

○ Will this be a waste of my time?

○ Will I be sorry I agreed to see her?

It's not only prospects who wonder about salespeople; it's just as common, and as big a source of relationship tension, when the seller is still wondering about the prospect. Your anxieties and your questions are the flipside of those your prospect has. Here's what you're thinking about before your first contact or your first face-to-face...and for long after, if you fail to address them:

○ Is he gonna be a jerk? Or worse?

○ Why did he agree to see me in the first place?

○ What's his hidden agenda?

○ Will he give me the full 45 minutes I asked for?

○ Are we going to be interrupted by calls or e-mails every three minutes?

- Will he answer my questions honestly, so I can gather the knowledge I need to really be of help, or will he be feeding me disinformation, thinking he'll gain the upper hand in some later negotiation over price?

- Does he care about anything other than price?

- Will he respect my expertise?

- Will he play mind games or make me jump through hoops?

- Will he listen when I'm speaking?

- Will he be so boring that I'll have trouble staying awake when he's speaking?

- Does he know his own job and his own organization well enough to be a good client and a good partner in the selling process?

- Does he have the juice to make a decision, not just on my final proposal, but on anything?

- Will he deliver on promises he makes to me?

- Will this be a waste of my time?

- Will I be sorry I ever called on him?

Just as your prospect is unlikely to mention his concerns, you're unlikely even to think about yours, even to admit to yourself that you have these concerns, that they're all too real. You focus instead on your agenda—the capabilities presentation, or the product demo, or the needs-assessment questions you'll ask—as you put your game face on, press the elevator button, and head up to meet him.

LACK OF OXYGEN

Both of you enter that first appointment with hope, or else you would never have agreed to set aside time to meet. But you also enter with all those questions, concerns, doubts, and anxieties. The questions persist, whether you're greeted warmly and offered a cup of coffee, or whether you get a cool or distant welcome. The questions remain, hanging heavy in the air, because no one ever talks about them, no one ever addresses them, no one ever deals with them. But those questions are the source of relationship tension, the bad cholesterol that obstructs the flow in your sales arteries. Relationship tension makes even the simplest thing sound, look, or feel awkward. Your question sounds a little stiff and stilted. His answer sounds short and tentative. One of you steps on the last words of the other, as happens so commonly in conversation between friends, but here it causes an uncomfortable moment, followed by a clumsy recovery— because you're not friends. You're strangers, and the tension in the room reminds you of it, over and over.

> *Relationship tension makes even the simplest thing sound, look, or feel awkward.*

TWIN CURVES OF TENSION

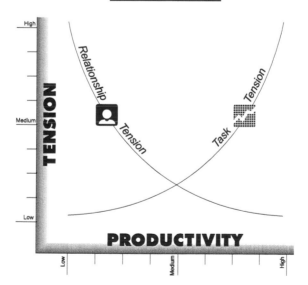

That's relationship tension. As the Twin Curves of Tension graph shows here, when *relationship tension* is high, productivity is *low*. But when *task tension* is high, productivity is *high*.

Plainly put, you can't get serious about the business issues until you have each other figured out. So it's in your interest—and your prospect's, no less—to take action to reduce the relationship tension that's so heavy it's sucking the oxygen out of the room. Until you do, that glorious task tension will not flow. Until his questions about you and your questions about him are answered—satisfactorily—relationship tension will smother any hope of doing business. There will be little trust. Communication will be guarded at best, perhaps even hostile, suspicious, and dead-ended. As long as the buyer and the seller are guessing about each other's true objectives and agendas, wondering about each other's credibility and trustworthiness, the sale is going nowhere. A small percentage of initial calls never experience this kind of tension, and another small percentage work through it and survive. But unresolved relationship tension—and therefore, *unrealized* task tension—remains the single biggest reason why there is no second appointment, and there is no sale. It's really a multi-billion-dollar embarrassment because the problem is so preventable.

The problem is unresolved expectations. The solution is to resolve them. In Chapter 4, you saw how common and easy contracting is in your personal life. You simply need to carry that everyday behavior into your sales life, and understand that you can contract about more than just time and place. Contracting—addressing and aligning expectations—is all around us every day. It's happening when a TV station flashes a message before a program starts, warning you that the content may be unsuitable for young children and giving you a chance to change the channel or switch the set off. It's happening when you see a sign at an amusement park for the "Raging River Rapids" ride. In smaller letters at the bottom it says, "Riders will get wet...possibly even soaked!"

What do you suppose is the sign's purpose? You're thinking of two different purposes, aren't you? The additional information at the bottom of the sign makes Raging River

Rapids even more enticing to those seeking an adventure and some relief from the summer heat, so long as they're dressed to get wet. And of course it's there to forewarn potential riders about the perils of getting tossed about in a little rubber raft with waterfalls overhead. By making it clear in advance what people can expect, the sign helps reduce any discrepancy between customers' expectations and their subsequent experience.

What might happen to Raging River Rapids if it failed to post the sign? It would be guilty of creating a yawning *expectation gap*. That expectation gap might cause:

- Large groups of wet, angry people to resent the company and their experience with it.

- Soggy, unhappy customers to tell others about their experience, thereby spreading negative word-of-mouth advertising and poor perceptions about the company.

- The company to lose clientele—or go out of business altogether.

- The company to find itself the defendant in a bunch of lawsuits.

So the sign goes up. The company is protected, and customers—those who choose to ride and those who don't—are a lot happier.

YOUR TURN

Can you post a sign outside the room where you'll be having your first appointment with a new prospect? Not literally; the world's not ready for that. But there are other ways to communicate expectations (and they work better than posting a sign, because the sign is one-way communication). I'll show you the *interactive* way to do it.

But let's imagine for a moment that you *can* post some sort of sign your prospect will see before the meeting. What would it say? What expectations would you state? Think now about one specific appointment you've already set with a new prospect. Or if you have no suitable appointment on your calendar just now, think of a specific new prospect with whom you should be making an appointment in the next week or two. You must have a specific account in mind, or this personal workshop won't come alive for you. Once you've selected the prospect you'll use, write down every expectation you have for an upcoming call on this prospect. Begin creating your own "expectation sign" by jotting notes on a sheet of paper. Here are some questions to help get you thinking in the right direction (feel free to go beyond these questions; they're just thought-starters):

- How long do you expect the meeting to run?
- How important is it that you are not interrupted during the meeting?
- What is the purpose of the meeting? What's on your agenda?
- What's *not* on your agenda for this first meeting?
- What do you expect the outcome of the meeting to be?
- What's the benefit of this meeting to you, the seller?
- What's the benefit of this meeting to the prospect?
- Who do you expect or wish to be present at the initial meeting?
- What will your role be, and how do you expect to relate to the prospect during this meeting—as an equal, as an expert, as a buddy, what?
- What do you hope will be the feel and the flow of this meeting?

You already have a longer list than you had expected, right? Once you've finished writing notes in response to these questions, take it a step further. Generate a list of *every* expectation you have for the meeting, including anything you're *wishing* for, *wondering* about, or *worrying* over. Make the list as long as you can. Don't worry about whether or not these are expectations you'd feel comfortable sharing. For now, just write it all.

Know that your prospect has a list similar to yours! But he hasn't written it all down. He hasn't given it nearly as much thought as you have, and he won't—until and unless you invite him to. But while he's only semi-conscious about his own list of expectations, they are powerful nonetheless. They lie in wait—ready to open up a big expectation gulch, ready to turn your appointment sour—not because he's a bad guy who wants the meeting to fail, but just because no one is paying attention to expectations.

Sandra, Jack, and Brian

When you've finished your list, keep reading to find expectation lists generated by Sandra, Jack, and Brian, three salespeople you'll be getting to know....

Sandra sells for PromoGold, a company that markets multimedia sales promotions, from concept to execution. Sandra's objective when she meets with Tom, a divisional sales manager, is to get a project assignment so that she can come back with a compelling proposal.

Here is what Sandra is *wishing*, *wondering*, and *worrying* about:

- I want to meet in their offices, and I hope to get an uninterrupted hour so that we can get below the surface and into some real depth.
- I hope they'll do most of the talking—and I hope they'll be totally candid about what promotional resources they can and cannot bring to the table.

- I want to let them know how we're different from other promotion companies they may have worked with in the past, and the unique way we work with our clients.
- I want them to understand that I'm here to help them solve one of their tougher problems—but NOT one of their impossible ones!
- Tom's counterpart—the divisional marketing manager—really ought to be there too.
- I hope it turns out to be a lively two-way exchange of ideas and possibilities. I sure hope they'll be creative and open-minded.
- I gotta let 'em know that everything discussed will be kept completely confidential.
- I want to be sure to share with them some new tools we've developed to improve the targeting of campaigns and promotions.
- I hope they won't stonewall me when we get into discussing their slower-moving lines.
- I wonder what specific expectations they will have about this meeting...

Jack sells for FleetServ, a GMC and Mack truck dealership that provides fleet sales, leasing, and maintenance services. Jack's objective in meeting with Wendell is to learn about value-added opportunities so that he can submit a proposal not focused exclusively on price.

Here is what Jack is *wishing, wondering,* and *worrying* about:

- I really want this meeting to happen at their Northpoint Distribution Center...and I hope at least half the time we can be walking around the garage, the lot, and their service and parts center.

- I'm gonna ask for 30 to 40 minutes—but I hope we end up going an hour longer than planned!
- I want to avoid getting trapped into talking specs, prices, terms, and bids, and focus instead on how they use their fleet and what their specialized needs are.
- I need to let 'em know I have a zillion questions.
- I hope Wendell won't be looking at his watch a lot.
- I won't be wasting his time...I hope that becomes clear quickly.
- I hope we hit it off and have a natural, easy-going conversation—not stilted.
- I'm gonna get one of my most satisfied customers to call Wendell in advance (hope he appreciates that).
- I want him to understand that my purpose in this appointment is not to come away with a deal.
- I can offer fresh perspectives based on my day-in-day-out conversations with fleet managers from all over the region.
- I might even be able to find solutions for some fleet problems he may have figured were impossible to solve.
- Ultimately, I want to be able to present, not an off-the-shelf lease and servicing package, but one designed specifically for Wendell's company and its fleet.
- I gotta find out his expectations too....

Brian sells for CustomNet, a firm that designs and installs custom computer networks for small businesses. Brian's objective when he gets together with Sally and Jan is to demonstrate his capabilities well enough to be allowed to conduct an on-site survey.

Here is what Brian is *wishing, wondering,* and *worrying* about:

- The appointment has got to take place in our Network Capabilities Center and I should ask for the customary 45 minutes.

- It's really critical that Sally makes it for this meeting—her vote counts more than the rest in selecting a vendor.

- I wanna blow 'em away with our technical capabilities and then segue smoothly into a discussion of their company, its systems, its customers, its competitors, and its current and future needs.

- I sure hope Sally grabs the mouse and starts to control the pace and the direction of the presentation. I'm twice as likely to win the contract when that happens.

- I hope they reveal who we're up against.

- I'd rather they speak to two or three of our competitors first, before I get my shot with them.

- I can help them make some discoveries about the tremendous potential of the information they've already gathered in their business...gotta remember to tell some stories about what some of our customers have accomplished using the custom network solutions we've created for them.

- Only finalists will be able to go the next step, conducting a formal on-site survey of their systems and their needs. I want to be one of those finalists.

- Be sure to ask Jan—maybe even Sally?—what their expectations might be.

The lists generated by Sandra, Jack, and Brian are comprehensive and wide-ranging. They take into account a broad variety of expectations—and some pure wishes too. Of course, not all of the expectations on these lists are ones they, or you, can contract for. But as you'll soon see, it is quite possible to contract for a lot more than time and place. Every time you contract successfully, you've made your relationship more interactive, you've behaved like a partner, and you've prompted your prospect to become a partner too.

Kudos to these three salespeople. Each recognized that his or her prospect has expectations too, and each noted on paper how important it is to ask the prospect to express his or her expectations. You haven't made it interactive, if you lay your expectations on the other person but fail to inquire about his.

> You haven't shared control and accountability if you lay your expectations on the other person but fail to inquire about his.

Interactive selling starts before the first interaction! Partners are already thinking about expectations, and how to manage them, before they ever pick up the phone, send an e-mail, or drop a note. If that sounds a little obsessive, pay attention to the wisdom of Marcus Manilius, a Roman scribe who penned this nearly 2,000 years ago: *Finis origine pendet.* Translation: The end depends on the beginning. Instinctively, we know this is right, which is why—outside the sales realm—we naturally look backward to find the root cause. If we see someone is having a bad day, we ask them, *Did you get up on the wrong side of the bed this morning?* If a software program is outputting nonsense, an IT geek will surely remind us, *Garbage in, garbage out.* You can't place too much emphasis on *getting started on the right foot,* to quote yet another aphorism that reminds us how much the end really does depend on the beginning. When you're finding a particular prospect hard to close, your problem is not the Big Close staring you in the face, it's all the little closes you failed to achieve earlier. You should obsess about expectations, and plan to manage them, from the moment you first start thinking about that prospect. It's how the pros close—early and often!

CLOSING THE CHAPTER

I believe these are some of the key takeaways from this chapter:

- The two types of tension are similar to the two types of cholesterol—one needs to be lowered and the other one raised.

- *Task tension* is the intensity, power, and direction you feel when you and your prospect are fully focused and moving forward, when you're so in the flow that you lose track of time.

- *Relationship tension* blocks your sales arteries, keeping both of you out of the flow because you both have unanswered questions—unresolved concerns, anxieties, and doubts—about working with each other.

- As long as relationship tension remains high, task tension cannot grow, the business relationship cannot develop, and the likelihood of a sale is small.

- *Contracting*—addressing and aligning expectations in an explicit and fully collaborative way— resolves relationship tension and opens the door wide for task tension to develop.

- The end invariably depends on the beginning.

What really rang true for you in this chapter? What did you find yourself taking notes about, or highlighting in your favorite color? What do you hope never to forget? I'd love to know. My e-mail address is SteveMarx@InteractiveSelling.com, and please put "Chapter 5" in your subject line.

CHAPTER SIX

MINI-CLOSING: LITTLE AGREEMENTS LEAD TO BIG DEALS

CONTRACTING EXPECTATIONS IS A NATURAL PROCESS ALL of us unconsciously use repeatedly throughout the day. It's high time every salesperson learn how to magnify his or her everyday contracting into *interactive selling,* into mini-closing, and learn how to close like the pros.

You're contracting—executing little agreements, mini-closes—all day, every day. When you phone your spouse and say you'll be late for dinner, you're contracting. When you warn your 8-year-old that next time there'll be punishment, you're contracting. When you tell the waitress that you need to be finished in time for the 7:40 movie, you're contracting. It's a shame how many salespeople fail to make full use of this powerful, familiar, and obvious process when working with clients and prospects. These little agreements create trust and engagement, they lead to slightly bigger agreements about agenda and process, and then on to much bigger agreements about doing business together. This is *interactive selling* at its most fundamental level. In this chapter, you'll learn just how to contract expectations—yours and theirs—and in succeeding chapters, you'll learn the rest of the practices that make you a partner.

In Chapter 5, Sandra, Jack, Brian, *and you* each created a "wish list" of expectations, desires, wants, and needs for an important upcoming appointment. Your list, as was theirs, is for a meeting with a prospect with whom you're still very early in the process, and perhaps have not even met before. I encouraged you to add some outlandish wishes to your list, even though they may not be things you can contract for, at least not so early in your relationship with this person. But you'll see that you can go a lot further than merely confirming the time and place of your appointment, and that when you do, trust and engagement develop faster and better than ever before.

On the following pages, you'll again see the wish lists put together by Sandra, Jack, and Brian. But this time, they have crossed out those items they believed they could not address with a prospect they barely know yet.

SANDRA:
- I want to meet in their offices and I hope to get an uninterrupted hour so that we can get ~~below the surface and~~ into some real depth.
- ~~I hope they'll do most of the talking and I hope they'll be totally candid about what promotional resources they can and cannot bring to the table.~~

- I want to let them know how we're different from other promotion companies they may have worked with in the past, and the unique way we work with our clients.
- I want them to understand that I'm here to help them solve one of their tougher problems—but NO T one of their impossible ones!
- Tom's counterpart—the divisional marketing manager—really ought to be there too.
- I hope it turns out to be a lively two-way exchange of ideas and possibilities. I sure hope they'll be creative and open-minded.
- I gotta let 'em know that everything discussed will be kept completely confidential.
- I want to be sure to share with them some new tools we've developed to improve the targeting of campaigns and promotions.
- I hope they won't stonewall me when we get into discussing their slower-moving lines.
- I wonder what specific expectations they will have about this meeting...

JACK:

- I really want this meeting to happen at their Northpoint Distribution Center...and I hope at least half the time we can be walking around the garage, the lot, and their service and parts center.
- I'm gonna ask for 30 to 40 minutes—but I hope we end up going an hour longer than planned!
- I want to avoid getting trapped in talking specs, prices, terms, and bids, and focus instead on how they use their fleet and what their specialized needs are.

- I need to let 'em know I have a zillion questions.
- ~~I hope Wendell won't be looking at his watch a lot.~~
- I won't be wasting his time...I hope that becomes clear quickly.
- ~~I hope we hit it off and have a natural, easy-going conversation—not stilted.~~
- ~~I'm gonna get one of my most satisfied customers to call Wendell in advance (hope he appreciates that).~~
- I want him to understand that my purpose in this appointment is not to come away with a deal.
- I can offer fresh perspectives based on my day-in-day-out conversations with fleet managers from all over the region.
- ~~I might even be able to find solutions for some fleet problems he may have figured were impossible to solve.~~
- Ultimately, I want to be able to present, not an off-the-shelf lease and servicing package, but one designed specifically for Wendell's company and its fleet.
- I gotta find out his expectations too...

BRIAN:

- The appointment has got to take place in our Network Capabilities Center and I should ask for the customary 45 minutes.
- It's really critical that Sally makes it for this meeting ~~her vote counts more than the rest in selecting a vendor.~~
- ~~I wanna blow 'em away~~ with our technical capabilities and then ~~segue smoothly~~ into a discussion of their

company, its systems, its customers, its competitors, and its current and future needs.

- ~~I sure hope Sally grabs the mouse and starts to control the pace and the direction of the presentation. I'm twice as likely to win the contract when that happens.~~

- ~~I hope they reveal who we're up against.~~

- I'd rather they speak to two or three of our competitors first, before I get my shot with them.

- I can help them make some discoveries about the tremendous potential of the information they've already gathered in their business...~~gotta remember to tell some stories about what some of our customers have accomplished using the custom networks we've created for them.~~

- ~~Only finalists will be able to go the next step, conducting a formal on-site survey of their systems and their needs. I want to be one of those finalists.~~

- Be sure to ask Jan—maybe even Sally?—what their expectations might be.

Having generated and now fine-tuned their expectation wish lists, Sandra, Jack, and Brian are ready to contact, confirm, and contract:

Contact. You must contact your prospect in order to contract expectations. A live contact (possibly in-person, but preferably on the phone) is by far the best, but if you know that your prospect is active and engaged on e-mail, that's your second choice.

Confirm. Contracting expectations is part of confirming the details of your appointment, so it invariably begins with a recitation of the date, time, and place of your meeting. It's important to understand that contracting expectations is *not* a new buzzword for "getting the appointment." Contracting is about creating an understanding of what shape the meeting will take—after you've already secured the meeting. Your local bookseller has lots of books that include a chapter on how to secure appointments; in fact, you've probably already read a few of them! This book doesn't go there. *Close Like the Pros* is only about how to add interactive selling to the good sales practices you're already using. That said, you might get some new ideas here about how to entice a new prospect to meet with you—consider that a bonus for being an astute reader!

Contract. Your management of expectations follows the confirmation of date, time, and place, by just one short breath. You'll see how Sandra, Jack, and Brian do it. Typically, this contracting happens at the tail end of the conversation in which you nailed the appointment, though it may happen later.

Now let's listen in as our three sales pros actually convey their expectations for that all-important first meeting—and note how, in each case, they invite the prospect to share his or her expectations too.

SANDRA OF PROMOGOLD:

> *Okay then, Tom, I'll meet you at your office Wednesday at 2 p.m. I understand you'll try to have the divisional marketing manager present as well. I've set aside an hour for this meeting and I'm hoping you'll be able to get away from your phone for that hour so we can stay focused and get into some depth. I'll talk a bit about how working with PromoGold is a little different from working with some of the firms you've dealt with in the past. I also want to be sure to share with you some new targeting tools we've developed. Mostly, though, I want to hear about your marketing and sales promotion hassles, challenges, and opportunities so that I can be of the most help. Meetings such as this are*

usually lively exchanges of ideas and possibilities—of course, everything you share with me is kept completely confidential. Before we hang up, I'm wondering if there are any other expectations you have for our meeting.

Tom's Response to Sandra:

That sounds fine, Sandra. I'll reserve the conference room and ask my assistant to hold my calls. We can't go quite an hour, though. I have to be walking out the door by 10-of-3.

Jack of FleetServ:

Thanks for finding 30 or 40 minutes in your schedule for our meeting, Wendell. I'll see you Tuesday at 10 a.m. at Northpoint, and I'll be sure to enter at Gate 5. I've got a bunch of questions about how you use your fleet, what your lease needs are, and the kinds of changes you're looking to make in your new position there. Just so you know, though, my purpose is not to come away with a deal from this meeting...we don't work that way. We've got no off-the-shelf lease and servicing packages—everything's designed specifically for each customer's needs. As you and I walk around the garage Tuesday, I'll have a chance to learn about those needs. Even if nothing comes of these conversations, I think you'll benefit from the time we spend together, because I can offer some fresh perspectives from my daily conversations with other fleet managers. How does that all of this sound to you?

Wendell's Response to Jack:

I'm glad you mentioned the other fleet managers. I'm curious to know just who else in the state you folks work with, so I hope you'll have a complete list you can leave with me.

BRIAN OF CUSTOMNET:

> *I look forward to meeting you at our Network Capabilities Center, Jan, and I'm glad to hear that Sally is able to attend. We'll have the coffee brewing Thursday the 22nd at 8:30 a.m., and we'll probably have you and Sally out of there by 9:15. I really urge you to speak with two or three other custom computer network suppliers before we get together...you'll be able to ask tougher questions that way and keep us on our toes! We'll actually be using a network to demonstrate what our network capabilities are, and then I want to move into a discussion of your company, systems you're using now, your customers, your competitors, your current and future needs, and the like. From what I know already, you've amassed a tremendous amount of information in your database, and I want to show you how the correctly designed network can leverage that information. Is there anything else you or Sally would suggest to ensure that this meeting will be a good use of your time?*

JAN'S RESPONSE TO BRIAN:

> *Not really. Everything sounds good to me, Brian. I'm quite excited to see what you have there!*

As you can see, these contracting efforts are little monologues, typically about 30 to 40 seconds long—*perhaps the most important half-minute in selling.* They don't become interactive until the end, at which time the salesperson asks the client or prospect some sort of question intended to bring out *whatever* expectations he or she may have.

THE CONTRACTING TURNS INTERACTIVE

It's essential that you ask the prospect for her expectations. Find your own way to ask the question, but keep it *very broad* so the prospect understands that you are seeking *whatever expectations* she may have about the meeting or about your business relationship, not just certain kinds of expectations such as agenda items. If you fail to conclude your expectation-setting monologue by asking the prospect for her expectations, then you've sent a strong and dangerous message: *Now you've heard my expectations, but I'm not interested in hearing yours.* So dropping this question about the prospect's expectations will undermine the partnership, instead of jump-starting it.

Are you surprised at some of the expectations Sandra, Jack, and Brian contracted? Most salespeople leave almost all of these things unsaid—as if they are either unimportant or unaddressable. They are neither. Leaving them unsaid keeps both seller and buyer in the dark, to no one's advantage.

It's not contracting at all if you fail to ask the prospect for his or her expectations.

When Brian asked Jan for her expectations, she had nothing to add. You'll encounter that sometimes. But both Jack and Sandra did learn about expectations of which they were not previously aware. Sandra learned that Tom had to leave after 50 minutes and that his schedule was not flexible. That's important information. It might alter Sandra's pace or priorities; more importantly, when Tom rises to leave at 10 minutes before 3 o'clock, Sandra will not be left wondering if perhaps he was making an excuse just to get out of there! Jack learned that Wendell was especially focused on seeing FleetServ's client list. Armed with that information, Jack could make sure he brought one along, not something he typically has with him on a normal call. (Jack hates to walk in with a big briefcase jammed with anything the prospect might ask for.) Because Jack took the time to ask, Wendell not only got the information he was seeking earlier than he otherwise would have, but of even greater value, Wendell learned that Jack was focused as much on Wendell's agenda, interests, and priorities as he was on his own. Jack bought himself a lot of trust and goodwill, just by contracting expectations, long before he ever met Wendell face-to-face.

When you ask your client or prospect to share his expectations, you're a lot more likely to hear what's truly on his mind—what expectations need to be managed. Yes, it's true that some prospects are plenty assertive when it comes to making their expectations explicit, but many others are not. And you sure can't close every expectation gap unless both of you know *where the gaps are.* What the sales pros know, that so many others still do not, is that when you invite the prospect into the process by mutual contracting of expectations, even the most assertive of them feel a bit less of a need to assert themselves! Perhaps most clients have learned to speak up for themselves—sometimes even jump up!—because that's the only way to get the bulldozer's attention and declare their interest in playing an active role in the sale. When you're contracting, right from the word *go,* the prospect figures out pretty quickly that you truly care about them and their issues, and that you intend to be an equal partner with them.

Few prospects will *initiate* contracting. It's as unusual a move for buyers as it is for all but the best sellers. Until interactive selling becomes more widespread in the business world, don't wait to see if your prospect "wants to contract." He wants to—he just doesn't know that he should, or that he can. When it comes to contracting, he's just like you were before you picked up this book! Contracting is *your responsibility.* I guarantee that your clients and prospects will follow, because they recognize instantly that it's in their best interests for everyone's expectations to be addressed and aligned.

Don't wait and see; it's your responsibility to initiate the contracting.

Each time you express your expectations, and the other person expresses hers, and you resolve any differences or discrepancies, you've just made a little contract. It has no dollar value, there will be no invoice, but it's a deal, nonetheless. It's a little agreement on the way toward a big one. It's a *mini-close* that engages the prospect, shares control, jump-starts the buying, and puts both of you on the interactive path.

IT FEELS AWKWARD THE FIRST TIME

Just as the first time you sat on a two-wheeler when you were five years old, contracting is going to feel a little awkward at first. Soon it will become as indispensable to selling as your "wheels" were to getting around the neighborhood. It won't take much practice or rehearsal before contracting becomes less awkward, less daunting—before it becomes as comfortable as those old boat shoes you've had for who knows how long. Most people to whom I've taught contracting have found it helpful to write some notes or even a full script the first time (or first several times) they contract expectations with a client or prospect. It rapidly becomes second nature, but many people continue to jot some brief notes beforehand, just so they won't forget something important. I do.

You'll quickly discover that, even though you're feeling a little clumsy delivering your first contracting monologue, your prospect is remarking to himself how very poised and professional you are, how much you seem to be taking his interests and his agenda into consideration. Moments later, you're listening to him turn your monologue into a dialogue as he naturally contracts right back to you.

YOUR TURN

Look at your calendar now. Find your next two appointments that are your first call on those two prospects. If you don't have two initial sales calls on your calendar at this time, then use the name of a new prospect with whom you plan to be scheduling an appointment very soon. Enter those two names in the spaces at the top of each column. Now think about those calls and answer the following four questions for each one, by circling either MORE or LESS in each statement:

PROSPECT NAME:

PROSPECT NAME:

If the prospect knew my real purpose in wanting this meeting, he or she would be **MORE** LESS likely not to cancel on me or stand me up.

If the prospect had a more accurate idea of the kinds of subjects I'm planning to bring up, he or she would block out **MORE** LESS time for this meeting.

If this prospect better understood why I do business the way I do, he or she would be looking forward to our meeting with **MORE** LESS enthusiasm.

If I were to reconfirm in advance not only the date and time of this meeting, but also the content and goal of the meeting, this prospect would consider me **MORE** LESS professional.

If the prospect knew my real purpose in wanting this meeting, he or she would be **MORE** LESS likely not to cancel on me or stand me up.

If the prospect had a more accurate idea of the kinds of subjects I'm planning to bring up, he or she would block out **MORE** LESS time for this meeting.

If this prospect better understood why I do business the way I do, he or she would be looking forward to our meeting with **MORE** LESS enthusiasm.

If I were to reconfirm in advance not only the date and time of this meeting, but also the content and goal of the meeting, this prospect would consider me **MORE** LESS professional.

Were you able to answer **MORE** all eight times? If not, I would suggest that you're not ready to make those calls yet. If you're not clear about your agenda, what value you'll bring, and how the appointment will benefit the prospect, it will be hard for him to see the value too. But if you are clear, and you agree that MORE is the right answer throughout, then it's time to practice contracting expectations.

You've seen how Sandra, Jack, and Brian took their lists of anything they were *wishing* for, *wondering* about, or *worrying* over, pared them down to those things they believed they could, at this time, address with their prospect as a specific expectation, and then executed their *contracting monologue* over the phone. Now it's your turn to go through that same process.

Begin with the wishing-wondering-worrying list you wrote back in Chapter 5. Now that you've read here in Chapter 6 how our three sales pros handled the contracting for their initial call on a prospect, are there any other expectations you would like to add to your list? Review your list and make any additions to it now.

Once your list is ready, the next step is to cross out any item that might be inappropriate to contract for at this early stage in your relationship. But don't scratch out everything but location, date, and time! As you saw with Sandra, Jack, and Brian, it's not only safe, it's also smart to address a broad range of expectations. Here are some of the expectations I've seen the pros close before that first call:

Duration. How much time do you need? How much will you ask for?

No interruptions. The prospect may not agree to hold calls, but can't you ask?

Purpose. This is probably just a simple statement, not a lengthy explanation, such as: *I have a lot of questions*, or *I hope to find out some of the major needs you have right now,* or *I want to talk with you about the unique way we work with clients.* Be candid and direct.

Nonpurpose. Saying what you expect *not* to do is a very strong and clear way of saying what your call is and is not about. For example: *We might spend an hour together and I might not even mention products, specs, features, benefits, or pricing,* or *I won't be asking you for a commitment—it's way too early in the process.* Your prospect may be very relieved to hear that, or she may be disappointed and tell you so. You certainly want to know, don't you? The process of agreeing that you either will or will not be discussing those subjects is contracting—addressing and then aligning your and her expectations. And with that one little agreement, you've set yourself on a course of interactive selling and buying.

Type of relationship. It only takes a phrase or two somewhere in your contracting monologue to communicate how you expect to interrelate with your prospect, for example: *working together* or *mutually explore* or *a two-way exchange of ideas.*

What's in it for the prospect. He's giving up time in a busy day for you. Let him know that you understand that, appreciate that, and intend to deliver value during this appointment (or conference call or online meeting), even if you end up not doing business. You might mention *sharing ideas,* or offering *a fresh perspective from someone who deals with a lot of different businesses,* or *so we can ultimately design something that's specific to your situation, not an off-the-shelf package.* This truly is your intent, but he may not realize it. So you need to address it.

Something specific. In some cases, you will have something quite specific that you wish to discuss on that call. As long as it is something the prospect will clearly be very interested in—because it revolves around his world, not your products or services—this is a great time to mention it. One short sentence.

Prospect's expectations. Here's where your contracting monologue becomes a dialogue. If you don't conclude your recitation of your expectations with a request to learn about the prospect's expectations, you're not contracting at all, you're dictating. Sandra said, *Before we hang up, I'm wondering if there are any other expectations you have for our meeting.* Jack said simply, *How does all that sound to you?* Brian's way of inviting the prospect to join the contracting was, *Is there anything else you or Sally would suggest to ensure that this meeting will be a good use of your time?* Whichever way you choose to ask the prospect for her expectations, make sure it's a broad question that the prospect can carry in any direction.

Write your contracting monologue now. If you work better from notes than from a script, then just write notes. When you're finished, rehearse it out loud and time yourself. It's nice to fit your monologue into 30 seconds; consider 40 seconds your absolute maximum. I'll give you extra credit if you write a second contracting monologue, this one for a different prospect you'll be meeting with for the first time in the near future. You'll see that there can be significant differences in what you contract, depending on the prospect and the circumstances.

Sales professionals who discover contracting remind me of kids when they first discover kissing: Once they find out how powerful it is, they want to keep doing it as often as possible. Once you see how contracting and mini-closing energize your selling—how it makes you the prospect's partner and the prospect your partner—you will look for more and more opportunities to share control and accountability with your prospect or client. You won't contract as often as *necessary*...you'll contract as often as *possible*. That's what Chapter 7 is all about.

The pros contract as often as possible, not as often as necessary.

CLOSING THE CHAPTER

I believe these are some of the key takeaways from this chapter:

- Contract expectations with a brief monologue, typically 30 to 40 seconds long. *Always* make it a dialogue by asking the prospect or client for her expectations.

- Contracting is your responsibility to initiate. Don't wait to see if the client wants to contract. Lead him there—he'll be delighted you did.

- Jot yourself some notes before important contracting, so you won't forget anything. The earlier you start making a list of expectations to manage, the better the list will be.

- It will be a bit awkward the first few times you do this. Don't skip steps while you're learning this. Make a very comprehensive *wishing-wondering-worrying* list. Then cross out those items you don't think you can contract for, and finally write yourself a little script.

- Each time you successfully contract, that is, set expectations collaboratively with the client or prospect, you've achieved a mini-close. You're measurably closer to doing business.

- Close like the pros—contract as often as *possible*, not as often as necessary.

Given the kind of selling you do, what were *your* big takeaways? Which messages in this chapter spoke loudest to you? Or which ones prompted questions or concerns? I want your feedback. E-mail me at SteveMarx@InteractiveSelling.com, and write "Chapter 6" in the subject line.

CHAPTER SEVEN
CONTRACTING IS THE NEW CLOSING

CONTRACTING IS A LOT MORE THAN GETTING AN IMPORTANT meeting set up correctly. It's the entire *expectation management* process that the pros use at almost every turn—before meetings, during meetings, and between meetings. Contracting shrinks expectation gaps and gulches right down to zero, wiping away most of the confusion, disappointment, mistrust, and conflict that characterize so many failed sales efforts. You'll see productive *task tension* ratchet up, and both of you will be so focused and so in-the-flow that ideas, opportunities, and possibilities will multiply. Prospects will want to meet with you again—"because this is going somewhere," they'll say.

You're gradually accomplishing the sale, and they're gradually making the purchase. And more meetings mean more *contracting*.

Once you discover the power of contracting, you won't just do it as often as *necessary*; you'll do it as often as *possible*. At a minimum, if you want to close like the pros, you'll contract at the beginning and end of every meeting with a client or prospect, whether it's on the phone or in person. Here are examples of some other times contracting will be your go-to solution:

○ When you sense confusion, surprise, anxiety, or disappointment creeping in (yours or theirs).

Bob, I sense that in the last few minutes you've become distracted or preoccupied with something. Has this become an inconvenient time for you to finish this meeting? Is there a problem I can help with, or would it be better for us to pick this up again, say, tomorrow?

○ When you sense an expectation gap opening up.

Hi, George. I see you brought your attorney. Hello, Hank. George, I thought today's meeting was going to be just between the two of us. I'm pleased to work with both you and Hank, but had I known Hank was going to be here, I would've brought Joyce, my company's attorney. Was I mistaken in my understanding?

○ Before you open a potentially sensitive subject of discussion.

I have some questions about volume and profitability for each of your recently introduced lines, Kathy. Understanding these numbers will make it much easier for me to tailor my proposals toward the best opportunities for adding incremental profit. I know we haven't worked together very long yet, but I want to assure you that we treat this kind of data and market intelligence with the utmost confidentiality. I hope you're comfortable going there.

❍ Whenever you feel a need to clarify where you are and where you're heading.

Kevin, I see a puzzled look on your face, or maybe it's concern about what I'm going to do with the information if you answer my question about your competitive strategy as openly and sincerely as you'd like to. A candid answer will help us design a solution that will generate the marketplace advantage you're seeking. I can assure you that everything you say to me will be held in strict confidence. That's how we do business.

Contracting is a pause in the content, designed to focus briefly on the process to ensure that both parties are still in sync, still sharing control, still feeling comfortable with where and how things are going. Contracting keeps the partnership path clear of weeds and twigs, not to mention logs, boulders, and quicksand.

By this time, our pros Sandra, Jack, and Brian are well into the interactive selling-and-buying process. After several successful meetings with their prospects, there's evidence all around that there could well be a very healthy order just over the horizon. And they're still contracting. Let's eavesdrop on each of them as they continue to address and align expectations about both content and process. As they did when we listened in earlier, each of them concludes his or her contracting monologue by inviting the prospect to participate, to share his or her expectations, to indicate if there's anything about the seller's expectations that doesn't quite jibe with his or her own.

SANDRA OF PROMOGOLD (SPEAKING AT THE CONCLUSION OF A MEETING):

> *Just to review the agenda, Tom...you and Joan can both make it Friday morning at 8. I will have Rich— one of the two retail promotion specialists you met last week—with me. Rich and I will focus on three possible promotional partners he has been research- ing in depth. Rich is enthusiastic and full of ideas, and sometimes gets more than a little exuberant...but that keeps things fun around our offices, and I sus- pect it'll keep the meeting lively as well. You will have the dealer information your staff has been collecting, and I'll have some very preliminary cost estimates. I understand we can't go beyond 10 min- utes of 9, so we'll have to keep the forward pressure on. Is all of this consistent with your expectations?*

JACK OF FLEETSERV (BY E-MAIL, BETWEEN MEETINGS):

> *Last week, I think we both started getting frustrated at all the interruptions...they made what should have been a 30-minute meeting last for close to an hour and a half. I'm hoping you've come up with a solution for that problem. When we get back to- gether next week, I want to propose something a little out of the ordinary. You'll tell me if it's a pos- sibility or not. It would involve putting one of our own factory-trained service techs out at Northpoint for as many as five evenings a week. I'll also have a lot more information about a seasonal payment plan to smooth out cash flow, as your CFO had re- quested. I'll be there Wednesday at 11 a.m. at your main office. Do you have any other needs or expec- tations I should know about?*

BRIAN OF CUSTOMNET (BY PHONE, PRIOR TO THE NEXT MEETING):

Jan, let's take a minute to discuss the on-site system survey and figure out how we can make it go as smoothly as possible. At some point during the day Tuesday, I'll need you and Sally each for a half-hour or so. Please also schedule two telemarketing reps, two customer service reps, and two people from the fulfillment department for 15-minute interviews each. While all of that is going on, Jackie—whom you haven't met yet—will be observing your people as they work. Occasionally, she may ask them to go offline for a few minutes, so if you anticipate a busy day, you might want to schedule a couple of extra people so customer service doesn't slow down. Please talk to your people in advance and make sure they understand that Jackie is not evaluating them or their performance; she's only studying the system and how it works. Do you have any concerns about this plan, or any other expectations you want to discuss?

As you can see, some of the contracting Sandra, Jack, and Brian were doing was very routine and mundane. But not all of it. Jack was annoyed at all the interruptions last time, when Wendell kept taking calls. Yes, some prospects are that way, but if you let it be known, in a nice way, that you would prefer they hold those calls or let them go to voice mail, many prospects will respect your request and get it handled.

> The deeper you are into the sales cycle, the less mundane the contracting is.

Sandra wanted to be certain that Tom was prepared for the slightly off-the-wall guy she would be bringing along next time, so she decided to mention that in advance, so that Tom might see Rich as "fun" rather than weird.

Brian decided, based on some past experiences, to ask Jan to assure her people prior to the site visit that Jackie was observing the technology and the process, not evaluating anyone's performance. In each of these cases, the salesperson was endeavoring to head off possible problems by setting expectations and ensuring a smooth process at the next meeting.

Contracting gets everybody's expectations out into the open and then *addressed* and *aligned*. It's not something you do just once, before you first meet with the prospect. It's something you do frequently, because content and process are always changing, expectations are always evolving, and the partnership is strengthened every time you purposefully share control and decision-making. So every time you express your own expectations, it's essential that you ask the other person to express hers.

Clients and prospects don't always agree with your contracting monologues. That's okay—that's why we're contracting in the first place: to *seek* agreement where it may not already exist. Perhaps it's just the wrong day, time, place, or agenda you've suggested for the next meeting. If there's a defect in your expectations, you want to fix it *before* the meeting, not during or after. Sometimes the defect runs deeper. Never fear hearing *any* sort of no, any type of push-back, any kind of curveball. Fear *not* hearing it. Fear not learning about it until long past the point at which you could do something about it. Fear not learning what your prospect was really thinking until after you've "thrown good time after bad," until after you've wasted time and energy with the wrong prospect, the wrong person, or the wrong project.

Fear only what you don't hear.

One of the greatest virtues of continuous contracting is that, while it strengthens some relationships and makes the sale more likely, it also points clearly to trouble brewing in other situations, giving you the choice of trying to rehabilitate that relationship and put the sale back on track or walk away from your investment before you sink any more time, sweat, or resources into it. When you're contracting at every opportunity, it's like you have a meter plugged into the sale, and the needle is indicating how solid you are with that prospect.

YOUR TURN

Roll up your sleeves again. It's time to write another contracting monologue, but this one will be different from the one you wrote earlier. Look ahead on your calendar, this time for a scheduled appointment with a prospect you've gotten to know from prior meetings. Or it might be a client you've known for years. Choose an appointment that's not routine, in which there is some risk that everything might not go just as you're hoping. It might be:

- A prospect who e-mailed you a day or two ago to let you know that there's a new regional manager assigned here, and that he may drop in when you're there next Wednesday.

- A meeting with an existing client who's been very pleased, for a number of years now, with the product, service, or application he's been buying from your company—but now that product is being discontinued, and the alternatives you have available are quite different.

- A situation in which, during your most recent meeting, the prospect told you a competitor had been in, offering a lower price, and you realize now you need to rebuild the solution you'd been developing with the prospect, in order to meet a lower price point.

- The follow-up to a meeting that really didn't go all that well. You're wishing now that you knew about contracting a few weeks ago, but you didn't,

and that call had more than its share of sour moments. But you do have another call scheduled,
and this one needs to go much better.

So choose a situation that is anything but routine, and is
no slam dunk. Think ahead to that meeting, and jot yourself
some notes about everything you're *wishing* for, *wondering*
about, or *worrying* over. Think about the usual content and
process items: duration/interruptions, purpose/nonpurpose,
relationship/atmosphere, benefit to prospect, specific content/
topics, and of course, the prospect's expectations. Don't be limited by these categories. Keep writing possible topics for contracting this very important upcoming meeting.

When your list is complete, look it over, and cross out the
items you really can't contract for, or those you won't have
time for in a contracting monologue that runs 30 to 40 seconds. Then prepare a script, or make yourself some speaking
notes, and lastly, rehearse it out loud and run a timer to make
sure it's not too long.

Now that you've prepared this contracting monologue for
that high-stakes call, will you use it? Let me ask you the question another way: If you used it, would it make it more or less
likely that the call will go as smoothly as you hope?

YOUR HEALTHY SALES DIET: CONSTANT CONTRACTING

By now the benefits of contracting are becoming obvious
to you, along with the hazards inherent when you fail to manage expectations. The *interactive sellers*, the pros who close
more deals and bigger deals, never stop *addressing* expectations and *aligning* them. For them it is a healthy habit, a routine with as great an impact on their sales results as your morning
jog and your whole-wheat-toast-and-hold-the-butter breakfast has on your fitness and longevity.

Interactive salespeople contract expectations for each appointment at least twice:

○ At the end of the conversation in which they have secured the appointment, as an extension of their confirmation of time and place.

○ Optionally, if and when they reconfirm the appointment.

○ At the beginning of the meeting, when of course there is no need to include time and place, but every other piece of the contract should be repeated, and the client or prospect's expectations should again be sought.

Interactive salespeople continue contracting as necessary during the course of a meeting, should the need arise, and they are always certain to contract once more as the meeting is drawing to a close. There are two general subjects to contract as the meeting is ending:

○ Who will do what between now and when. This is what I call *homework assignments*, and I'll explain them in Chapter 8.

○ Content and process for the next appointment. This contracting will, of course, be repeated when that meeting gets underway.

Jon, a gifted sales manager I have known for years and a fine practitioner of interactive selling, requires his salespeople to continue the contracting *post-appointment*. Within 24 hours of completing any in-person sales call, they must draft a "recap" e-mail. Each recap follows the same formula:

1. Thanks for the meeting.

2. A priority-order listing of the opportunities uncovered.

3. Who's doing what and by when.

4. A request for confirmation that all of this is consistent with the prospect's understanding. (*Did
we get it right?*)

Jon says these e-mails are "prompt, accurate, concise, and
engaging...and very effective!" Jon points out that e-mail is a
natural tool for this kind of contracting because everyone involved on the client side and the company side can easily and
quickly be copied.

The basics of contracting can be summarized with the
Five Ws:

WHO: It's *your* job to initiate contracting; if you don't do
it, it's likely no one else will. It's also your responsibility to
ensure that both of you are engaged in the process of addressing and aligning expectations, closing any gaps or gulches
before anyone gets hurt.

WHAT: Contract for both *content* (agenda, task, focus,
outcome) and *process* (methods, paths, styles, responsibilities).
Anything either party is wondering about, worried over, or
wishing for might be a good subject for contracting. When
you fail to contract something important, you are making an
assumption—and you know what they say happens when you
assume: you make an *ass* of *u* and *me*.

WHEN: At a minimum, contract *in advance of, at the beginning of,* and *at the end of* every meeting with your client
or prospect, whether it's on the phone or in person. In addition, stop and contract during a meeting or between meetings
if you sense confusion, surprise, or disappointment; if you
notice an expectation gap opening up; or whenever you feel a
need to clarify with the prospect where you are now and where
you're heading.

WHERE: Contract everywhere: In person, on the phone,
even by voice mail, e-mail, and instant messaging. Because
contracting is about *mutual expectations* being *mutually managed,* live contracting produces the best results. But even if

you're managing expectations by e-mail, voice mail, or snail mail, you must make it mutual. Always conclude with an invitation for the client to respond (...*and please add or clarify any additional expectations you may have for this next meeting*).

WHY: Contract as often as necessary, and you'll see big improvements in client relationships and sales performance. Contract *as often as possible* and you'll capture the power of interactive selling and begin to close like the pros.

THE ABC RULE OF SELLING IS DEAD! LONG LIVE THE ABC RULE OF SELLING!

Most salespeople have come across the tired and shallow "ABC" bromide that says sellers should Always Be Closing. Those three simple words epitomize the sales rep the world has come to know and despise. This is the rep who makes a pest of himself by closing prematurely, closing inappropriately, closing constantly, and closing clumsily. As with the proverbial stopped clock that's right twice a day, this rep makes a few sales just because he happens to run one of his closing tactics past a prospect at the right moment—when the prospect is ready to buy. But this crude concept of selling has never been worth more than that broken clock. It's no wonder salesmen have been consistently characterized in our culture as hapless, inept, morally corrupt losers for the last 50 years. If you've read or seen a production of Arthur Miller's *Death of a Salesman* or David Mamet's *Glengarry Glen Ross,* two of the most highly acclaimed works of the American theater, you must have winced just as I did at their portrayal of the sales profession.

If you picked this book up looking for a juicy list of "closing techniques" perfected by the pros, by now you may have figured out you grabbed the wrong book! What the pros have figured out is simply that the infamous closing tricks and tactics of sales' storied history no longer work. They understand that today's buyers are sophisticated. A great many buyers have been to seminars in which they've learned how to recognize—and how to neutralize—every closing zig, zag, and hop ever catalogued.

But instead of throwing the old ABC Rule out the window, let's update it. The ABC Rule for the new millennium is *Always Be Contracting*. Contracting is the new closing. It's the only genuine, valid, and useful closing practice that exists. It sure feels good when you finally get the signature, take a deposit, and run back to the office to ring the big bell outside the sales manager's office. But the pros know that the moment the prospect touches his pen to the paper is nearly a nonevent. Sales professionals recognize that they scored no dramatic victory that day, but rather that they scored a great many small victories in the days, weeks, and sometimes months prior, which led them to the surprisingly matter-of-fact moment when the prospect became a client. There's less drama and excitement the day the order is confirmed because the sales pro saw it coming so clearly. You see, the close was 95 percent *done* before the sun ever came up that day.

> *The moment the prospect touches his pen to the paper is nearly a nonevent.*

MINI-CLOSES MAKE MOLEHILLS OUT OF MOUNTAINS

As salespeople, we tend to dwell on how difficult it is to sell in these competitive times; what we often forget (until we go to buy a car, a house, a big-screen TV, or some other large purchase) is that it's also tough to buy. Think about the bewildering number of options available in almost every product category today. Consider the conflicting claims and boasts coming at you through a variety of media, promotional literature, and sales pitches. Ponder how yesterday's apples-to-apples comparisons have morphed into today's apples-to-kumquats. The risks inherent in making a poor choice make buying *tough*, and if you think it gets any easier when it's someone else's money (the company's), you haven't walked very often in the buyer's shoes. Corporate decision-makers don't have to defend their purchase only to themselves or their spouse; they have to defend it to their boss, their boss's boss, and perhaps The Board.

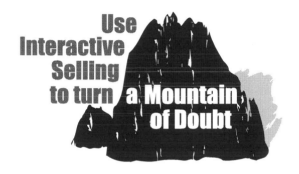

into molehills of decision

sequential, logical, incremental decisions

The sales-cowboy in some of you might be willing to try to lasso that customer-steer when he's still too far away, thinking you have little to lose. Save that macho stuff for your summer vacation at the dude ranch, where you probably do have little to lose. Even if you think *you* don't need to move incrementally, *you* don't need to mini-close your way to the deal, *you* don't need to get a lot closer before you use the lasso, *your prospect does.* He faces a mountain of doubt that begins when he decides to invest time and effort with one salesperson and not with another, or with three sales reps but not the other five.

The fact that you have budgets and goals to meet this month and this quarter is *your* problem, not the prospect's. If that's what's driving your actions, your prospect will sniff you out as fast as he'll smell a fish carcass rotting in his garbage can. Your mission is not to step up the pace, but *to be in the room,* and to be the prospect's trusted partner when those incremental decisions are being made. Your competitors who aren't using interactive selling are probably not going to be in the room, but you will be.

Your mission is not to step up the pace, but to be in the room.

There, you and your prospect are working collaboratively, because contracting is something you do *with* (not *to*) the prospect, on his schedule and consistent with his agenda. Few prospects can be rushed, few deals hurried up by popping the proposal prematurely. But every prospect can be helped, and every buyer can be assisted with making a good decision, one increment at a time.

A pundit once said the way to eat an elephant is one bite at a time. We all know how much easier problems are to solve when we break them down into their component parts. Most salespeople deliver a premature proposal loaded with surprises and devoid of prospect sweat-equity. They can earn either a big yes or a big no, and it's a lot safer for a prospect filled with fear and doubt to give them the no. In sharp contrast, the interactive seller is contracting and mini-closing at every turn, putting no mountains in the prospect's path, presenting him only with molehills—with logical, timely, sequential, *incremental* decisions—with opportunities to say yes or no to pieces and parts of the proposal as it is coming together. By the time the *interactively written* proposal is ready, the decision is largely made. The prospect feels empowered not bulldozed, confident not worried. The result is a big yes, built on countless yes and no decisions along the way.

Each mini-close secures a path, a direction, a concept, a price range, a timetable, or a set of particulars. Ultimately, mini-closes secure the partnership and the order (or the stream of orders). Every properly contracted meeting you have, every homework assignment, every half-baked idea, every trial balloon, and every progress report is an opportunity for a buyer and seller either to strengthen and deepen their evolving partnership—or to break it off. Each time a buyer chooses to go forward, he's that much more invested, that much more committed, and that much closer to awarding you the business. By the time you're ready to deliver your formal proposal, nearly all the closing should be behind you—and your prospect. If there is any "technique" to closing, it's simply that you and the prospect have been closing this deal together since the day you first met!

> *Each mini-close secures a path, a direction, a concept, a price range, a timetable, or a set of particulars.*

If the prospect wants to break it off, that's some of the most valuable feedback you could get. Welcome it. It presents you with three options:

1. **Ignore the feedback.** Pretend you never heard the prospect backing away, never noticed her wanting to wriggle her way out. Keep your fingers crossed that everything will be okay in the end. Continue investing your time and resources,

oblivious to the growing evidence that this is going nowhere.

2. **Dig in and find out why she's backing off.**
There's one or more issues driving her behavior,
and you'll have to deal with them (or suffer them)
at some point in the future. It's always better to
do it now. Perhaps you can fix it; maybe you can
solve the problem and put the project and the
prospect back on the path. Find out.

3. **Agree with the prospect not to "throw good time
after bad."** Fold your tent, knowing there are better prospects out there more deserving of your
investment right now, and knowing too that this
prospect may be a better investment at some other
time and in response to some other need.

If you follow the *new* ABC Rule—Always Be Contracting!—
you will never be confused with *Death of a Salesman's* Willy
Loman. You'll be seen as the salesperson who makes buying
easier, who helps the prospect with his purchase decision by
turning his natural *mountain of doubt* into consecutive, logical, incremental *molehills of decision.* Although it's true that
contracting is the new closing, it feels to prospects to be the very antithesis of closing. Prospects *welcome* and *embrace* contracting as
predictably as they build their defenses against
closing. That's because contracting is a collaborative series of steps that help the buyer deal
with the complexities and intricacies of decision-making, while closing just pressures them
to act prematurely. Turning the mountain of
doubt into molehills of decision is how the pros close. They
know something the average salesperson has yet to learn: Selling may be tough, but so is buying. By turning the mountain
into molehills, the salesperson has made the sales job easier
for herself and the buying job easier for her prospect.

Prospects welcome and embrace contracting as predictably as they build their defenses against closing.

CLOSING THE CHAPTER

I believe these are some of the key takeaways from this chapter:

- Contracting is *not* something you do once, at the outset, and it's set for all time. Constant contracting keeps all parties in sync.

- Minimum contracting is at the beginning and end of every meeting. At the beginning, you contract content and process for the meeting. At the end, you contract who will do what, between now and when.

- Contract—address the process and the relationship—whenever you feel confusion, surprise, anxiety, or disappointment—or you sense that your prospect may be feeling it.

- Don't fear hearing some disagreement when you lay out your expectations. *Fear not hearing it.*

- Contracting gives both parties an opportunity briefly to reevaluate where things are headed. Perhaps a slightly new direction is better, or maybe this is the moment for one or both parties to admit that their time would be better invested somewhere else altogether. The sooner you know, the better.

- Update the ABC Rule: Today it means Always Be Contracting. Contracting is the only genuine, valid, and useful closing practice under the sun.

- Few prospects can be hurried, but every one can be helped. Turn your prospect's mountain of doubt into consecutive, logical, incremental molehills of decision.

◑ Contracting is *the new closing*—but it feels to
prospects to be the antithesis of closing, because
you're continuing to share total control with them.

That's my list of the major concepts in this chapter, but what's
on your list? And what's on your mind? I really want to know.
Your feedback helps others, and theirs will help you, whenever
you visit InteractiveSelling.com. So please e-mail me with your
thoughts...at SteveMarx@InteractiveSelling.com. Put "Chapter
7" in your subject line.

CHAPTER EIGHT

THE MAGIC OF ASSIGNING HOMEWORK

HOW MANY TIMES EVERY WEEK DO YOU LEAVE A REASONABLY good meeting with a new prospect and ask yourself: *Is she really a likely buyer? I got nods and smiles, but I've seen those from prospects many times before. She asked a bunch of questions, but that's no sign this is heading toward a sale, either. How much time and effort should I continue to invest with her? Is there a big pot of gold for me at the end of this rainbow, or will it all be for naught?*

You need to learn the value—the magic—of *homework assignments*. They're one of the key *interactive selling* tools you have, and one of the best ways there is to integrate buying into selling. Aside from their immense value in *involving the prospect* and *improving the proposal,* they're usually the best way you have to measure whether or not the energy you are expending on a prospect is likely to lead to a sale. Should you redouble your effort—or punt? Homework assignments often tell you.

Prospects give off signs all the time about how truly interested they are in this product, this service, this provider, this proposal, or this salesperson. But it's easy to miss the signs. If the prospect is accepting and completing your assignments—or even better, is making assignments—things are on track and your time is well invested with this prospect. Pour it on, partner! If not, then you need to decide if there is something you can do—now!—to reengage the prospect and reinvigorate the process. Or if you should consider investing your time and resources elsewhere.

> **Should you redouble your effort—or punt?**

Sarah is a pro who understands and uses homework assignments as a matter of routine. Let's watch her in action:

At 3:15, Sarah began gathering her papers together and putting them into her briefcase. The meeting with Irene Brown had gone very well; it looked as though Irene was interested in bringing her company into Supplier City's Corporate Co-op, and Sarah could almost smell the large order Irene was talking about placing.

"So you'll check with Joe in marketing and give me the names of your company's five representatives for Supplier City?" Sarah asked Irene, restating the facts they'd agreed on earlier.

"Yeah," said Irene, glancing at her watch.

"I'm sure I can have the application forms sent to you by the end of next week, at the latest. I'll also put together a list for you of the other local companies your size that've been in the Corporate Co-op for more than six months. I'll include the list with the application I'll be sending you," said Sarah. "Can I expect to have those names and phone numbers from you by then?"

"Mm hmm," mumbled Irene distractedly, standing up and extending her hand.

"Okay then," said Sarah, also standing. "It was a pleasure meeting with you. I'll call you at the end of next week for those names."

As Sarah left Irene's office, she felt a little twinge of uncertainty. Irene had seemed interested in her company's programs and their networking trade association, the Supplier City Corporate Co-op, but she seemed sort of noncommittal about doing what was necessary to take their relationship to the next step.

Sarah was glad she had followed her usual habit of assigning some sort of task—homework—to her prospect. It had always been an early signal to Sarah of the prospect's true level of interest.

"I'll know if she's serious about working with us by the end of next week," Sarah thought to herself. "If she doesn't follow through with what she's promised—and if she doesn't fill out the applications I've committed to send—then I'll know where I really stand with Irene, and I'll have some decisions to make."

As she neared her own office, Sarah formulated her next steps. "I'll prepare the applications and the list of companies and send them out today," she thought. "Then, on Wednesday, when I'm sure Irene has received them, I'll call her and see if she has any questions. I can ask how her name-gathering is going and gauge her interest in continuing our relationship."

Sarah hasn't given up, nor should she. But she's got all her antennae up and tuned into Irene's frequency. She's watching and listening for signals. So far, the message coming through the static is hard to decipher, but Sarah fully expects, within a week or so, to have some clarity. Sarah is an optimist by nature, but experience has tempered any tendency she may have had toward cockeyed optimism, and when it comes to how she uses her most precious resource—her time—Sarah is an optimistic realist.

IS HE OR ISN'T HE?

You may be a lot like Sarah. You've learned quite a bit about a prospect, discussed his needs, and batted around a few ideas. Now you're trying to determine: Is he *really* a likely buyer? How much time and effort should I continue to invest with him?

The best way to find out is to assign homework—out loud—to yourself and to him, as early and as often as you can. The homework you assign to the prospect shouldn't be an onerous or time-consuming task; it should be something that's clearly necessary; and it should be just large enough to test your prospect's interest level and keep him actively participating. The importance of testing the prospect's interest level is just this: The acceptance and completion of homework assignments tells you quite a bit about your prospect's engagement, his optimism about doing business with you at this time, and his willingness to help you craft a proposal good enough for him to buy. Some people just like to talk, to learn, to confirm that the decision they're leaning toward—to go with your competitor—is really the right one. Homework assignments take you past the talk. Here's how they work:

 If the assignment is readily accepted, the prospect is showing clear, probably strong, interest.

 If the prospect completes the homework by the mutually agreed-upon date, you have an even stronger sign that you have a partner who's willing to work with you to make your proposal one he could buy.

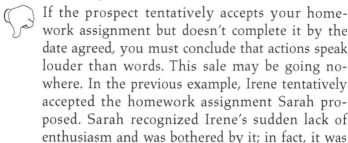 If the prospect tentatively accepts your homework assignment but doesn't complete it by the date agreed, you must conclude that actions speak louder than words. This sale may be going nowhere. In the previous example, Irene tentatively accepted the homework assignment Sarah proposed. Sarah recognized Irene's sudden lack of enthusiasm and was bothered by it; in fact, it was the cause of her "twinge of uncertainty."

If the prospect accepts the assignment, then fails to complete it, *but is chagrined and apologetic,* you may still be all right. Some people who do intend to be your partner might be too busy to follow through by the agreed date, which is why you're watching for the strength and sincerity of the apology. Be aware, however, that if this scenario is repeated, it could be a sign that the prospect is, at best, undecided about the value of investing in you and your proposal.

If the prospect easily accepts the homework assignment but later can barely remember it and isn't bothered by her failure to follow through, you'd better face facts: This deal is probably dead. And wouldn't you rather know now—before you invest more of your precious time—than later?

If the prospect doesn't even accept the homework assignment, the message is that he has little interest in being your partner. It's unlikely he'll become a large, profitable, and consistent client— or even that he'll end up making the one purchase under discussion now.

In the example, Irene, the buyer, initially seemed interested in the Supplier City opportunity Sarah was presenting; but, as Sarah noticed, something caused her to fade out and seem less interested as the meeting wore on. Maybe she was running late for another meeting or appointment, or maybe—just maybe—Irene had only agreed to meet with Sarah because she'd heard that one of her competitors had joined Supplier City and she just wanted to know what the competition was up to.

Whatever the reason for Irene's distraction, Sarah responded with a technique intended to gauge Irene's level of interest in their continuing to work together. She did that by assigning homework to Irene—complete with a due date:

"So you'll check with Joe in marketing and give me the names of your company's five representatives for Supplier City?" Sarah asked Irene, restating the facts they'd agreed on earlier. "Can I expect to have those names and phone numbers by the end of next week?"

It's not enough for Irene to *say* she has some interest in what Sarah is proposing; as we all know, that's a fairly effective technique used for getting rid of pesky salespeople. It's far more telling if Irene *proves* her interest by lifting a finger to move the process forward—not toting a bale, just lifting a finger.

But Sarah didn't stop there; she tested Irene's interest further by making an assignment to *herself* out loud. Sarah's assignment to herself was to mail an application form to Irene, compile a list of selected local companies involved in Supplier City's Corporate Co-op program, and then call Irene for the names of five people from her company who might serve as Supplier City representatives.

Sarah intentionally assigned herself the more complicated set of tasks and then waited for Irene's reaction to her assignment. She knew that Irene's response, be it positive or negative, would give her another way to measure how interactive this relationship is and how likely it is that a good sale awaits Sarah. In fact, announcing out loud all the homework you are taking upon yourself is equally effective as asking the prospect to do something. Decent prospects (which most are) won't allow a sales rep to invest blood, sweat, and tears in a proposal they know isn't likely to turn into a sale. Hearing all the work you plan to do on your prospect's behalf, she will nearly always speak up and slow you down. In this case, though Irene seemed a bit tentative, or even a little dismissive, of the one little piece of homework Sarah asked her to complete, she was silent when it came to Sarah's multiple assignments. She didn't slow Sarah down, so that's probably a good sign! Perhaps Sarah might have a good partner here after all.

Few prospects will allow a sales rep to invest blood, sweat, and tears in a proposal they know isn't likely to turn into a sale.

As it was the first time you contracted expectations with a prospect you had never met before, the first time you assign homework to a prospect and to yourself you may feel a little uncomfortable. It won't be long at all before you value the practice of assigning homework out loud and use it regularly to take the temperature of your sales relationships. On the next two pages you'll see flowcharts that describe the various ways in which prospects respond to homework you assign— and what that response might be telling you.

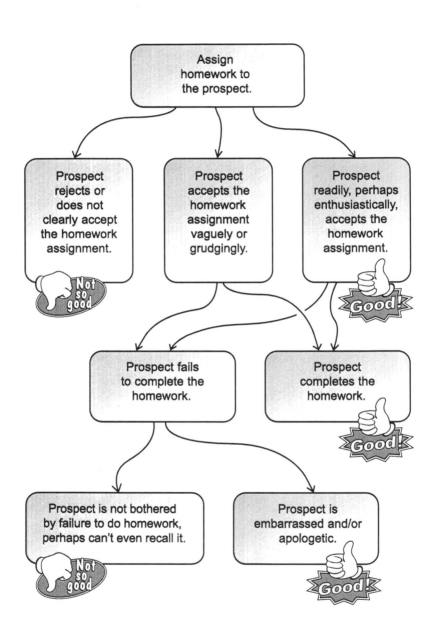

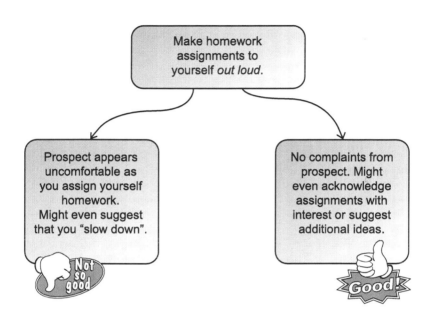

Make homework assignments to yourself *out loud*.

Prospect appears uncomfortable as you assign yourself homework. Might even suggest that you "slow down".

Not so good

No complaints from prospect. Might even acknowledge assignments with interest or suggest additional ideas.

Good!

It's your own little feedback loop. The more often you make specific homework assignments to both the prospect and yourself, the more information you'll get back as to whether or not this deal is heading toward success.

THE PROS TALK OUT ABOUT HOMEWORK

I love hearing sales pros tell me how well *interactive selling* practices work for them. Here are three who now employ the magic of assigning homework:

MIGUEL SELLS IN-STORE MUSIC AND MESSAGE SYSTEMS.

My existing customers are very loyal to me. They know I work very hard to provide them with great service and new ideas to help them. I'm a pleaser. And I'm a persuader—they sometimes tease me about that.

I have that same enthusiasm and desire to please when approaching prospects, but I know when to do how much. For example, I had targeted this big chain of retail stores, and my prospect Jane and I were talking about the regional managers and what outcomes they wanted to drive at the store level. It was clear that some input from those four people would really help the process along.

Other people in my company, they'd do it all themselves—you know, get the names and contact information for these managers and track them down to get their input. I used to do that too, before I figured out what really works. It sorta makes sense that the easier you make it on the prospect, the more likely they will buy from you. But it's not that simple.

What I said to Jane was, "Let's divide up those calls and get 'em all done between now and our meeting a week from Monday. I'll do two, you do two. Let's get their input on what they would like to get accomplished locally with a storewide music and message system." Jane thought about it for a beat or two before she answered. I know from experience this is a moment of truth. Will she or won't she? Does she want our plan to be as perfect as possible? I know it was only two or three seconds, but the first time you do this it feels like an eternity. Then Jane said, "Okay, I'll get that done. I'll have Carol give you the names and numbers of the ones you should call and I'll handle the others.' From that point forward Jane and I were working as partners, not salesperson and prospect. I don't know how much longer it would have taken to get to that point, if I hadn't asked her to do some homework.

DONNA SELLS LOGISTICS SOFTWARE.

When I first heard the concept of giving homework to a prospect, I think I laughed. It sounded like it was junior high school. When I stopped laughing, then it sounded awfully presumptuous. To say I was resistant to the idea of passing out homework assignments would be an understatement.

So here is what I did: I took the idea halfway. I started giving myself homework assignments. It was just a matter of telling the prospect exactly what I was planning to do—I didn't change my plans, all I did was stop keeping my plans to myself. I still remember the first time I did this. It was my second meeting with a huge trucking firm prospect. I couldn't tell how much progress I was really making, so I assigned myself the task of contacting each of his 11 depots to compile volume data, which is pretty routine for us. William, the IT manager I was dealing with, interrupted and told me not to do that—that it wasn't quite the time for me to go to that much trouble.

That was sobering, but it was also incredibly helpful. I just asked him why not. Turned out we ended up talking for another half hour or longer, as William told me all the stuff he hadn't told me before— and I realized he wouldn't ever have told me if I hadn't announced all my homework. I was sold on homework assignments from that moment on. William had had some very bad experiences in the past with other software providers. I took the time to get to the bottom of those of issues and I was able to help him feel much better about how my company deals with the procedures that put him in a tough spot before. By the end of the meeting, William repeated his instruction that I not contact those depots, but not for the same reason. He said he had all that data already and would run a report and have it ready next time we met.

I'm so sold on homework now, I assign it in both directions.

MERRILL IS A SALESPERSON WITH A TELECOMMUNICATIONS PROVIDER.

I've always prided myself on hard work. Nobody in my office handles more prospects and spends more hours every week putting together proposals than I do. I've done pretty well, but I noticed that a few others in my office were going home a lot earlier than I was and their volume was bigger than mine.

My new sales manager, Howard, opened my eyes. He pointed out that I was actually doing too many proposals and I needed to smoke out the time-wasters so I could concentrate more time and effort on the best prospects, the ones most likely to book. Howard showed me how to use homework assignments as a way to tell who might be serious and who's got a whole different agenda or is just too nice to say no.

I don't start doing the heavy lifting involved in drafting a proposal, and I sure don't get into pricing, until the prospects have some skin in the game. So I give 'em homework. I ask for a whole range of technical data, information I'm gonna need later on anyway. Some have the data at their fingertips— and hey, I don't need any homework assignment to know they're for real. But most have to provide it to me later. Do you know that half those people I never hear from again? And to think I used to put together a formal proposal for almost everybody!

For those who do get back to me, depending on the circumstances (sometimes it's the internal politics at their company), I may have more homework for them. Good prospects are more than willing to accept their assignments. All this work I have 'em do—it makes a better proposal. But the main reason I do it is it tells me who is a better prospect!

I told Howard thank you. I told him I'm doing fewer proposals now than I ever have, but I am doing more installations, and bigger ones. My volume is up by almost a third. I don't do proposals if the prospect doesn't make an investment. I don't have time for that anymore.

HOMEWORK IS NOT BUSYWORK

All three of those pros use homework assignments the way a doctor uses a blood-pressure cuff—to take a "reading" they might not be able to get any other way. But homework assignments have a secondary value that's nearly as important. Merrill pointed to it, saying, *All this work I have 'em do—it makes a better proposal.* While Merrill mentioned it, Miguel and Donna were also using homework assignments to further the work of developing the very best proposal, the best solution for the client, the one that would be easiest to buy.

If the homework you assign to your prospect is busywork, if it has no obvious connection to solving the prospect's problem, to meeting his need, to delivering value, you run two considerable risks. The first is that you might appear to be clueless about what's important to the prospect or to the proposal or both, and the second is that the prospect might decline the assignment, or fail to complete it, not because he's not interested in your forthcoming proposal, but simply because the assignment was insignificant or off-focus.

Use homework assignments the way a doctor uses a blood-pressure cuff.

Homework that's in-focus will be embraced by the prospect as worthwhile, as his opportunity to make an important contribution to the final plan he knows he'll be asked to purchase. That kind of homework brings buyer and seller closer, builds trust and interactivity, gets the buying to happen alongside the selling instead of in tandem, and *improves both the proposal and the prospect.*

Every time you prompt the prospect to become engaged at the level of a contributor to the evolving solution, you are tapping someone with access to information that would be difficult or impossible for you to gain by other means, including:

- ☉ Company's purchasing policies, purchasing history, and various purchasing constraints.
- ☉ Company's decision-making process and hierarchy.
- ☉ Company's culture, style, and structure.
- ☉ Role and influence of third-party suppliers, as well as other policies, programs, and priorities that might interface with or impact your proposal.
- ☉ Internal resources that can be tapped, as well as resources not available from within the company that must be supplied externally.
- ☉ What other people or business units are likely to benefit, to be impacted, or to be accorded influence over this purchase.

◑ Ways to expand internal resources or funds so as to expand the deal or amortize its cost over a broader base.

The more often you tap the prospect's information and influence, not only when you're face-to-face, but between meetings by assigning homework, the more viable—because it's more buyable—your proposal becomes. Every time you prompt the prospect to contribute, he is likely to prompt the same of others inside his company. These are all mini-closes, because the buying is happening while you're selling, one increment at a time.

Failing to use homework assignments—both as a system for engagement and partnering and as an *interactive selling* meter—is opportunity squandered.

Your Turn

Open your calendar. Find your *last three* in-person appointments, or if most of your selling is inside, then write down your *last three* substantial phone calls. For each call, write down at least two specific "out loud" homework assignments for yourself and one specific homework assignment for your prospect—assignments you either did make (congratulations, partner) or you could have and should have made. If you did not assign this homework while you were meeting with the prospect, can you do it now? These calls are still quite fresh; perhaps it's not too late to go back and make those homework assignments now.

Now look ahead on your calendar and find your *next two* scheduled appointments. It's not possible to know beforehand just how those appointments will go, but you probably have some idea of the agenda, or the prospect's needs, or the issues you're working through right now with that client. What sort of homework assignments might be appropriate to give to the prospect, assuming the meeting goes in the direction you anticipate? Make yourself some notes now, in advance of those appointments; you can always change your homework plans as you're wrapping up the meeting.

The homework assignments you're preparing for now are an essential practice for the interactive seller. Some of the benefits of assigning homework aloud include:

○ You provide the prospect with an unprecedented level of control in modulating the development of this relationship, making her more comfortable with you.

○ You prompt the prospect to continue her active investment of time, energy, information, and ideas. As her investment grows, the chance decreases that she'll decide to walk away from it (and you!).

○ You monitor the prospect's level of interest, engagement, and optimism about doing business with you.

○ You advance the sale incrementally, by advancing the purchase incrementally. Acceptance of homework and performance of homework are mini-closes, little molehill decisions along the path toward a business partnership.

Billions of dollars worth of time, effort, goodwill, and resources are wasted each year by salespeople who continue to cater to prospects who aren't going to buy. Homework assignments smoke them out—and enable you to invest in direct relation to your opportunity for return.

CLOSING THE CHAPTER

I believe these are some of the key takeaways from this chapter:

- ○ Homework assignments often tell you whether to redouble your effort with that client—or punt.

- ○ Acceptance and completion of homework assignments tells you about your prospect's engagement, his optimism about doing business with you now, and his willingness to help you build a proposal good enough for him to buy.

- ○ If the prospect is disengaged and not likely to buy, wouldn't you rather know now than later?

- ○ Homework assignments given to the prospect should not be onerous. *She doesn't have to tote a bale, just lift a finger.*

- ○ Assigning homework to yourself—out loud—is also highly effective at gauging the prospect's level of interest. Few prospects will let you invest blood, sweat, and tears in a deal they know is going nowhere.

- ○ Homework should *never* be busywork. It should always be an assignment that the prospect would need to contribute at some point anyway, in order to improve either the proposal or its execution.

- ○ Every time a homework assignment is completed, *it improves both the prospect and the proposal.*

Remember, you're welcome to e-mail me with your thoughts, your questions, your concerns, and your experiences. What points in this chapter stood out for you? Let me know (I read every piece of mail I get!). My address is SteveMarx@InteractiveSelling.com. Put "Chapter 8" in the subject line of your message.

CHAPTER NINE

HALF-BAKED IDEAS:
THE POWER OF UNDERSELLING

MUCH OF WHAT YOU KNOW ABOUT PRESENTING IDEAS TO your prospect is wrong. The "conventional wisdom" about how to package and present your idea isn't wise at all, but it sure is conventional—it's everywhere. The advice is told and retold so often people stop questioning it and just accept it as Revealed Truth. Here are some of the misguided notions about how salespeople (or anyone, for that matter) should present their ideas:

○ Present your idea with passion, power, and pizzazz.

○ Fill your presentation with color and detail, so your idea comes alive for your prospect or your audience.

◯ Work out all the particulars and how-tos in advance, so you won't be caught flat-footed by any question the prospect might pose.

◯ Don't leave anything to chance.

The pros don't work that way. They know that all that standard advice—which *seems* to makes sense—is just plain wrong. They're smiling as they read this because they know the conventional wisdom is not just less effective, it's exactly backwards!

Take those bullet points I just gave you and do a 180. Now you have the *interactive-selling* strategy of *half-baked ideas*. Yes, it's counter-intuitive; it seems crazy to think that presenting your idea without pizzazz and without particulars might work better. It seems weird to say that you're better off *not* thinking through all the details. On the surface, it may seem senseless to leave out the color, the flavor, all the reasons why your idea is white-hot. But that is indeed what the pros do. Sometimes they do it naturally and subconsciously; other times they do it with astute premeditated intent. They have a much easier time selling their ideas than you do—if your habit is to *do it up big*.

No pizzazz and no particulars. Half-baked ideas are instead interactive and collaborative.

Here is Sally's experience:

Volume Builders had been a client of Multimedia Events for several years. Training Director Donna Gladstone liked the quality of the PowerPoints, animations, videos, and participant binders Multimedia produced for her training seminars, and she liked the way Rob, her salesperson, always worked with her to make sure she got what she needed at the right price.

Sally had just taken over Rob's territory and was out to show her stuff—to demonstrate her value—to Rob's old clients. She invested hours researching each one, reviewing past activity, and devouring all the deliverables the client had bought in recent years. Then she applied her own creativity and experience to assemble a knock-their-socks-off proposal for each and every one. It was a lot of work, but Sally had something to prove to those clients and to her employer.

For Donna, Sally created a gorgeous trade show exhibit booth, because Rob mentioned before he left that Donna may be needing one. When Sally's booth ideas had finally been fine-tuned, problem-solved, and rendered in full color on 11×17 presentation boards by Multimedia's art department, she was ready to call Donna to schedule an appointment. She was put right through to Donna's office when she called Tuesday afternoon, and based on Rob's excellent service over the years, Sally was easily able to schedule an appointment for Thursday.

Sally arrived 10 minutes early for the appointment, toting her portfolio of renderings. She was psyched. And the appointment went perfectly. Sally rolled along, just as she had done the night before when she rehearsed at home. The meeting was made all the smoother by the fact that Donna had interrupted only once to ask one simple question.

Donna smiled as she rose to thank Sally for all her hard work. She asked for a few days to think it over, and whether she could keep the renderings, in addition to Sally's 28-page leave-behind proposal.

What Sally didn't know was that Donna is one of those cheery people who always has a smile on her face. In truth, Donna was just overwhelmed by the proposal. She really did appreciate the hard work, but everything else left her uneasy. The colors were wrong, now that Volume Builders had gone to the new logo and palette. The graphics were dramatic, and they used images that Donna had approved in past years, but they were not in any way interactive, and there was no video, which Donna knew she would need in order to be perceived as competitive with other exhibitors. Sally's walk-through design left no room for a conference table, and while the proposed lighting could certainly draw attention to the booth, Donna could only imagine how she and her team would be sweating under those intense lights.

Each of those problems was fixable, but that's not how Donna was thinking. She really wasn't able to focus on so many solutions—all she could do was think to herself, "This isn't how it was with Rob." She couldn't put her finger on the difference exactly, but she knew that there was a lot more give-and-take when she dealt with Rob, and she knew that Rob's ideas seemed spot-on while Sally's were all off-the-beam.

Donna needed some options. So she grabbed the Yellow Pages and looked to see who else was listed under Trade Show Exhibits.

Sally is in trouble with this account—and she doesn't even know it, which doubles the danger. She has taken a good client—one with whom she could readily schedule an appointment—and turned her into a tough prospect, one who did something she had not done in years: She invited a bunch of Multimedia's direct competitors in to pitch the business. Sally's in hot water here because she failed to partner with Donna. She learned about a need for a trade show booth and took it *to the max*. All by herself. She did it up big, when small would have been smarter. She was hyperactive, when she should have been interactive. Every time Sally added another element or feature to that booth design, she moved further away from a booth Donna would buy. More importantly, she *distanced herself* from Donna.

Sally did it up big when small would have been smarter.

How it might have gone

It's too bad Multimedia did not move Jenny into Rob's territory. Here's how her story would have played out:

Donna had been a client of Multimedia Events for several years. She liked the quality of the PowerPoints, animations, videos, and participant binders Multimedia produced for her training seminars, and she liked the way Rob, her salesperson, always worked with her to make sure she got what she needed at the right price.

That's why Jenny from Multimedia was put right through to Donna's office when she called Tuesday afternoon. After introducing herself and explaining that she was taking over Rob's territory, Jenny got to the point of the call:

"Before he left for his new position, Rob mentioned that you would be exhibiting at the international training convention next month. Is that still your plan?"

"Oh yes," said Donna, "I've been attending the show for the past three years. This will be my first year exhibiting."

"Then let me run an idea by you," said Jenny. "I haven't worked out all of the details, but I believe we can turn it around in time, if you think it's something you want to do.

"Because Multimedia prepares all of your materials, we have a lot of your custom graphics stored in our computers. Why don't we use those scaleable images to design some supergraphics for your booth at the trade show?" Jenny suggested. "We've created the images already, so the cost would be very reasonable, and you could pick and choose the graphics you want to use."

"Hmmm," said Donna. "Did you do a mock-up of the display you have in mind?"

"Not yet," admitted Jenny, "I think we need to sit down together and brainstorm some ideas first. One of our engineers, John Jacobs, has agreed to meet with us and then do some sketches."

"Okay," agreed Donna. "Let's meet Thursday of this week and talk about it some more—that'll give me a couple of days to sleep on it."

When the three sat down Thursday afternoon, Donna was visibly excited. "I've been thinking about your idea, Jenny, and I've decided to do it. What I'd really like, though—if we could manage to pull it together in three weeks—is more than graphics. I'd like a display that includes video, interactive technology such as I use in my training now, as well as printed information show-goers can take with them."

Jenny looked at John, who nodded. "No problem," he said. "Let's do some brainstorming...."

Is this kind of give-and-take typical of the proposal-generating process you use? If so, you're the exception. And if you partner with your prospects in this fashion, then you also know that:

- Jenny's process takes much less time than Sally's.
- Jenny spends more time with the prospect—and less time back in the office—than Sally does.
- Jenny's clients are less likely than Sally's to shop around.
- Jenny has an easier time fine-tuning the idea, because Donna is right there to smile or frown, right there to add her own input.
- Jenny is about 10 times more likely than Sally to get the order from Donna.

Jenny was using *half-baked ideas*. Half-baked ideas are one of the most powerful tools of *interactive selling*. Half-baked ideas invite the prospect in, instead of pushing him out. They prompt partnership.

The alternative is to Do It Up Big! Wax ecstatic and expansive early on. Build a dramatic and convincing presentation around your concept. Present it as if it were the greatest thing since Caller I.D., *without word one to—or from—the prospect*. Yes, it's another case of premature elaboration. When you sell that way, you have your head buried so far into your selling process that you are oblivious to the buying process that *isn't happening.*

Selling ideas, solutions, plans, and proposals that way is similar to proposing marriage on the first date. Or the second. How creepy is that? You need lots of dates, lots of time together, lots of environments and scenarios. Romantic dinners, trips to the mall, family visits, weekends at the cabin, a crisis or two, quiet times—you need all that and more

> *Don't be oblivious to the buying process that isn't happening.*

before you pop the question, and your significant other does too. Getting married is a big decision, and few people but Hollywood stars have ever made it quickly, or all at once. The way it really works is that we make *molehill decisions* along the way that move us toward the last molehill decision, the one that looks to everyone else like the Big Decision. Or sometimes those little decisions lead us away from this potential spouse, and ultimately toward someone else. It's an incremental process. Your first half-baked idea may have been just dinner and a movie, and it progressed from there. Sales is no different.

HYPE IS COUNTERPRODUCTIVE

The truth is, few ideas *are* the greatest thing since Thomas Crapper invented the porcelain throne. That fact alone should slow you down. Being told that an idea is fabulous doesn't make the prospect more likely to believe that it is; indeed, it may make him more skeptical. An enthusiastic presentation of an open-and-shut case, a complete-from-A-to-Z plan, causes most prospects to act like "show-me state" Missourians, to think you are, like Mr. Crapper's invention, full of feces. They say—verbally or through body language—*Oh yeah? Prove it!* Or worse yet, that's what they're thinking, but they're not saying a word.

Human beings are naturally suspicious of anything accompanied by even a *little* hype, and if that hype is coming from a salesperson, we put all our defenses on maximum alert. When you called the air conditioning company to come to your home for an annual inspection of your system, and the technician-salesman comes down from your attic, sweaty and grimy, with

We humans are naturally suspicious of anything with even a little hype—most especially when it's coming from a salesperson.

a trumped-up story about how you need to replace the entire apparatus or else your whole family will come down with Legionnaire's Disease, your hype sensor sounds an alarm. When a salesman puts you in a $500 Italian designer sport coat and tells you, "Now that coat is you!" and then grabs three shirts, four ties, and two pairs of trousers, and asks whether you prefer MasterCard or Visa, you retreat from the hype. A sunny disposition is helpful when dealing with anyone, but hype is never the sales pro's ally.

We've all heard so much hype from so many salespeople for so long. That's why most prospects these days look for what's *wrong* with a solution proposed by a salesperson rather than what's *right* with it. When the waiter pushes the $28 sea bass, you immediately start wondering if he was told by the chef to push it. *Did they buy too much of it?* you wonder. *Is it about to go bad? Or does it generate a higher profit for the house, so maybe there's an extra spiff for the waiter every time he sells one?* You're filled with doubt and suspicion. When the office furniture salesperson shows you a desk system that fits your measurements and notes your gentle nod and smile—and then tells you he can get you 20 percent off but only if you commit today—you recoil from the hard sell. The desk had seemed to be a possible solution for you, but the hype made you wonder why the salesperson thought letting you sleep on your decision might be risky for him.

The salesperson, by enthusiastically speeding along, by pushing the sale faster than the customer is ready to move the purchase, *creates* a tougher prospect and a tougher (if not impossible) sale. When the salesperson at the electronics store starts talking about the extended service warranty before you've even decided whether or not to go ahead with that expensive plasma TV, the message is clear. The seller is less interested in helping you choose the right TV for your home, and more interested in beefing up the sale with a high-profit-margin add-on. He's a selling-obsessed bulldozer, not a buying-focused partner. You know it in your bones, and you're less likely now than you were before to buy that plasma. Along the scale from zero to 10, where 10 rings the cash register, that salesman just moved you down to negative five.

Running out ahead of the prospect might be okay if all we had to do was sell. But the prospect also has to buy, and buying happens in increments. That's why half-baked ideas are so important. Our red-hot or white-hot idea really isn't so hot unless the buyer thinks it is. We can't know if it is or not, unless we're working alongside the prospect. Buyers make their purchase decision in stages, in increments. That's how they buy ideas and solutions: one part at a time. So that's how we need to *build* the solution and that's how we need to *sell* the solution. As Sally and Jenny demonstrated in our story, it doesn't take more time, but it does take more interactivity, more partnering, and more mutual idea-polishing.

> *Buyers make their purchase decision in stages, in increments. Get in sync.*

Some ideas are fatally flawed for a reason the salesperson could never have guessed: It might be a consumer promotion that would be perfectly okay for one client, but illegal for another client in a particular highly regulated industry. Or the idea might be to staff a call center with part-timers to handle peak hours, but the client has a policy against using part-time employees. Your idea might be to hand each female patron a red rose at dinner on Valentine's Day, but the owner's wife, who serves as hostess, is highly allergic to roses. Don't you just cringe at the thought of all the time wasted

preparing a proposal destined to go nowhere? All the time
you spent lining up that florist for the restaurant client....

THEY HAVE TO OWN IT
BEFORE THEY BUY IT

By presenting your thoughts as half-baked ideas—or even
one-quarter baked—you don't waste time or turn your prospects off before you've had a chance to turn 'em on. Prospects
love hearing ideas in the sketchy stage. They want to help
shape, develop, and fine-tune those ideas so they fit like a
glove.

Consider the contrast between Sally and Jenny: Sally
walked through Donna's door and handed her a finished proposal for a supergraphic display booth—with all the details
worked out, accompanied by elaborate sketches, and including a sign-right-here contract—and she turned Donna off.
Donna reacted by inviting competing companies in to bid. Even
if Sally's idea had been more on-target, Donna may have felt
bulldozed; with Sally doing all the leg-work, Donna would
have had no input into the design. The message implicit in
Sally's proposal was *I didn't need to get your input, your ideas
aren't all that important, our company wants to do it our
way, this proposal is take-it-or-leave-it, so why don't you take
it?* If you were Donna, you would have reacted the same way.
You'd push away...mentally, and maybe even physically. You'd
say *No!*

When the prospect doesn't "own" the idea or solution,
he's a lot less likely to buy it. Millions of sales proposals go
down in flames each year because the prospect was not invited to help develop the plan. Jenny was smart. She practiced
interactive selling. She sought Donna's input and allowed time
for it to happen. Jenny spent her idea-generating and -polishing
time not alone in her office, but shoulder-to-shoulder with
Donna, the person on whose decision the order hangs.

Ideas and possible solutions to problems ought to be trotted out as *early*—and be as *incomplete*—as possible. And they should be presented *hype-free*. Ideas and solutions should be presented in a vague, sketchy stage, with respect for—and a request for—the client's input and direction. Even an obviously terrific idea should be presented without endorsement, so the *prospect* can pronounce it terrific, instead of you!

And if the prospect doesn't think it's terrific, that's good too. Wouldn't you rather know now, before you invest even more time in it?

I call these deliberately incomplete and unfinished concepts *half-baked ideas* because our hope is that when we present this partially baked product, our prospect will finish baking it in his oven—my metaphor for the prospect molding and shaping the idea so it better meets his needs and capabilities, just as Donna did. Often we find that an idea will move back and forth several times between the prospect's oven and ours, each time getting closer to a solution that's both saleable and buyable. As the prospect contributes input and effort, the likelihood of a sale keeps going up, because *the prospect becomes fully invested* and because *the solution that's ultimately developed is better.*

As a salesperson, you have this simple choice:

Wow, wait' til you see what my people have come up with! They've really outdone themselves this time. You'll be really impressed when you see the plan we've put together for you!

We've brainstormed some possible solutions for you. I'd like to get your input on each of the five—so we know which ideas ought to be trashed on the spot, and which ought to be polished up for an immediate field test.

The hyperactive, selling-obsessed bulldozer makes the close a lot *tougher.*

The interactive, buying-focused partner makes the close so much *easier!*

Note, in the right-hand circle, that the interactive seller talked about "possible solutions." He didn't label his ideas as "half-baked." *Half-baked* is a colorful term that reminds us instantaneously of the strategy and how to use it, but as a phrase, it's *just between us*. Out there, beyond the walls of the sales office, the phrase has a more common connotation: It means cockamamie, poorly thought-out, ill-conceived. Words that might work for you include: ideas, approaches, possibilities, options, concepts, thoughts, notions, sketches, works-in-progress, and "some things I've been thinking about." Call any of them "partially developed" if you like, just *not* half-baked.

SHARING THE POWER OF CHOICE

Ideally, several half-baked ideas and/or solutions might be presented at once, so your prospect-partner has the opportunity to pick the one or two that seem the most promising, the most worthy of more time in the oven. Clients and prospects almost invariably respond well to possibilities presented in the sketchy stage. They tell me it gives them more control over the outcome and that, sometimes, it's just fun to see into someone else's thinking. When you present several possible approaches, each half-baked or even one-quarter-baked, you provide your prospect the opportunity to reject the ones she can't or won't buy and to focus both of you on the ones with promise. Together you'll bring the best idea(s) to finished form, with each of you providing input based on your own expertise, your own information, and your own perspective.

Offering just one half-baked idea has some value—the prospect at least can say yes or no to it. But when you step forward with three, four, or five potential options, the advantages really stack up:

● You demonstrate your effort to think of solutions from many different angles, which shows both creativity and caring.

● By laying choices before the prospect, you add interactivity to the process, and you enhance the prospect's investment in the evolving proposal.

● You improve your ROI—your return on your investment of time—because the solution that finally emerges will be more buyable and more likely to result in a sale.

Whether driven by new technology, increasing competition, or other forces, customer needs these days are often more complex than in years past. As needs grow more sophisticated, so too do the solutions you offer. Your proposals, plans, systems, and installations are more likely than ever to contain multiple ideas and elements. To ensure you're really meeting client needs, and more importantly, to improve every element of the plan or solution, most should be presented first in half-baked idea form.

Suggest several half-baked ideas; not just one.

Half-baked ideas are not just a step in each sales cycle. Each and every aspect of the proposal is another opportunity for you to be an interactive partner—and to keep the prospect a partner. The use of half-baked ideas—along with *trial balloons*, covered in Chapter 10—is a trademark of the sales pro; it's how the pros close. Even when you think it's a good idea, your job is to present the idea and let the prospect tell you if it's good. Will all this collaboration slow you down, and slow down delivery of that proposal? Perhaps. But remember, slowing down the proposal—keeping the selling going as long as the buying is not finished—will usually *speed up* the yes you're seeking. Your aim is to deliver a *no-surprise proposal*—no surprises inside for the prospect, no surprises at the end for you.

Half-baked ideas are one of your most powerful interactive selling tools. Use them regularly, and you'll discover not only how the prospect will help you develop the proposal, but how the proposal-building process can help you develop the prospect. Put another way: *You and the prospect create a better proposal, while you and the proposal create a better prospect.*

YOUR TURN

Think of a current prospect, one for whom you are now preparing a proposal to present. Select one for whom you are not fully certain the business is going to go your way. Rather than rushing to deliver that final proposal on your next call—thereby risking a rapid no— think of ways to use the half-baked ideas strategy on the next call, so you can be a lot more confident you'll get the order on the following visit.

Take a few minutes now to write down three to five half-baked ideas you can present informally on your next call. You may already have one, the one you're hoping they'll buy. Brainstorm some more. What kinds of ideas might these be? In most cases, it will be a specific *application* of one or more of your products that relates to this prospect's specific problem, need, opportunity, or situation. Or perhaps it's a specific *implementation* that relates to how your prospect's company operates. In other words, your half-baked ideas should be about *how* to use your products or services, not more reasons about *why* to use them. Write those ideas now. Don't go into the detail; just write the big picture—a sentence or two. But make each one specific and concrete. Write as many possibilities as you can think of, then pare the list down to the three or four you're most eager to discuss with your prospect.

Present the idea half baked and let the prospect tell you if it's good.

When you bring your half-baked ideas to the prospect, remember to *undersell* them. Ask the prospect which one(s) look the most interesting or promising—and watch to see which one makes the prospect smile or causes her to lean in and ask questions. Once you see a spark, find out what intrigues her. *Why did you select that one? What makes you think that will deliver more value for you than the others? What would I need to do to that idea to make it perfect for you?*

> *Half-baked ideas are about* how to use your product or service, not why *to use it.*

You'll come away from that meeting with the framework for a plan the prospect is likely to buy. Put meat on the bones of that idea, and your proposal is twice—maybe three times—as likely to sell. You'll be thanking me for half-baked ideas, and thanking yourself that you slowed down and added one or two more meetings before submitting your final proposal.

CLOSING THE CHAPTER

I believe these are some of the key takeaways from this chapter:

- Much of what you know about presenting ideas to your prospect is wrong.

- Take the conventional wisdom about how to present ideas and stand it on its head. Now you see the power of *underselling*, the power of *half-baked ideas*.

- Few ideas are really worthy of a big buildup, a grand entrance, a granite pedestal. What makes them good is *mutual sculpting and polishing*.

- Most folks are suspicious of hype. Superlatives and fancy staging just make us standoffish. They put us on maximum alert.

- Buyers make their purchase decision in stages, in increments. They buy the idea or the solution one part at a time. So the pros *build* the idea and *sell* the idea one part at a time.

- Millions of sales proposals go down in flames each year because the prospect was not invited to help develop the plan.

- Ideas and possible solutions to problems ought to be trotted out as *early*—and be as *incomplete*—as possible. And they should be presented *hype-free*.

- *Half-baked* is a colorful term that reminds us instantaneously of the strategy and how to use it, but it is a phrase that should stay *just between us*. Don't use it when underselling your idea to your prospect.

- Offering just one *half-baked idea* has some value. But when you step forward with three, four, or five potential options—each one undersold—the advantages really stack up.

What ideas—half-baked or otherwise—seemed most important for you to remember from this chapter? What passages did you find yourself underlining or highlighting? It helps me to know. Please e-mail me your thoughts right now. Place "Chapter 9" in your subject line, and e-mail me at SteveMarx@InteractiveSelling.com.

CHAPTER TEN

Know Every No: Trial Balloon Everything

As the saying goes, there are two things you don't want to see being made—laws and sausages! But most everything else these days is moving toward transparency. If you've been involved in a real estate closing in the last decade, you know there are more statements, schedules, explanations, disclosure forms, information forms, and consent forms than ever. You walk away with writer's cramp. Every last detail is presented, made transparent. From the nutrition label on Hostess Twinkies to the requirements of the Sarbanes-Oxley Act...from the Website that allows you to track your FedEx package along every mile of its journey to a fine wristwatch's exhibition caseback that lets you view the delicate movement inside...the unmistakable trend is toward *transparency*.

Sales pros work transparently too. They know that when they work in the sunshine, when all their moves are open, obvious, out there, and *contracted*, they create the depth of trust that leads toward big deals with big customers. They know that when they clear every detail and collaborate on every development, they're able to present a proposal that's ready to be bought because the prospect has already decided on every piece of it, every part in it, and every party to it. The pros' process is totally transparent, and they deliver a *no-surprise proposal* every time.

Work in sunshine and build trust.

The no-surprise proposal demands that you run everything by the prospect ahead of time. The proposal you ask her to buy should contain nothing that would cause her to raise an eyebrow. Everything must be tested and approved beforehand. I like calling these *trial balloons* because it reminds me to undersell them, just the way the pros do. Sales pros float a suggestion—without endorsement, commitment, or passion— and gauge reaction. It prompts the very give-and-take that is at the core of interactive selling.

The context—both the deal you're trying to put together and the relationship you're working to build—will tell you how soft you need to be in making the suggestion. Often, there's no need to be gingerly. You can be matter-of-fact and routine in making your suggestion. *Your strategy is to seek approval or consent for all the details that will comprise the final plan*— so that it will truly be a no-surprise proposal. If you can't get consent or approval for a particular detail, you need to find out why and then rework the details so you can. This isn't brain surgery—it's just interactive selling.

Your trial balloons might be about quantity, delivery dates, payment terms, third-party involvement, testing methods, or any of a number of other possibilities, including, of course, in most industries, price or cost elements. Unlike the half-baked idea, the trial balloon is not likely to be the central concept around which your tailored solution is being designed—a concept that will require modification, adaptation, or configuration before becoming the solution. Rather, a trial balloon is a nontrivial detail or element of either the *plan* or the *process leading to* the plan; the prospect can accept it, reject it, or make an alternate suggestion. Every time he does, the buying process has moved forward again, and with your help and involvement. That's interactive selling.

Your prospect needs an opportunity to think about and "buy" every aspect of the proposal. The pros focus on that buying process—who has consented to what, so far—knowing that if they succeed in facilitating the purchase, the selling process will have taken care of itself. As business becomes more complex and technologies permit an explosion of options and permutations, our sales proposals naturally include a greater number of elements and details, more moving parts, higher levels of sophistication and complication, and a longer cast of decision-influencers. That explains why many selling cycles are longer than in years past. If you sell solutions that are much simpler, with relatively few pieces and parts and a shorter selling cycle, consider yourself lucky and know that you're probably the envy of your peers who must deal with a lot of complexity. But beware that technology and competition may soon bring to your doorstep the same perplexing permutations and options that have already come to characterize the sale of so many other products and services.

Any detail you fail to trial-balloon along the way is a potential hazard. Interactive selling is your strategy for delivering a no-surprise proposal that is ready to be bought the moment it's delivered. Every element within your plan that has not been approved in advance by the prospect—either formally or informally—can become a stumbling block. (If they didn't see it coming, even a small issue is big enough to trip over!) Every time you present such a surprise, you put the prospect in the legitimate position of needing to "think it over."

The more time she needs, the more plan elements and proposal details she must consider and evaluate, the more guilty
you are of *handoff selling*. The more work your proposal requires after it leaves your hands, the more of

Any detail you fail to trial-balloon along the way is a potential hazard.

the buying process takes place with you not in
the room—beyond your reach, your input, and
your influence. If you want to close like the
pros, replace handoff selling with *interactive
selling*, and trial-balloon *everything* in advance.

Trial balloons should include most anything concerning
the process. Here are a few examples:

○ Which individuals from your firm and the client's
ought to be included in the development process.
*Though I'll be your main contact at our company,
I think it would be helpful to have Ray, our engineer, sit in on the next meeting or two. Is there
anyone from your company that you'd like to
join us?* (Follow-up, if necessary: *What would his
role be in our conversations?*)

○ Suggestions of subcontractors or third parties
whose products or services might be included in
the plan.
*Doug at Micromaniacs has a unique chip that
would enhance the value of the packages you'll
ultimately be offering for sale. Why don't I ask
him to join us for a brainstorming session?*

○ Research or testing methods used along the way.
*I'd like to organize a focus group and get some
feedback from your customers before the product is finalized. How does that sound to you?*

○ Involvement of key decision-influencers, so they
too can be part of the interactivity.
*What do you think about getting Matt, your re-
gional manager, to come to town for our next*

meeting, as a way to build his support for the concept we've been working on here?

○ Concerns you've had, or sensitive issues that must be addressed at some point in the process.

I hear you make reference pretty regularly to the LogistiNet system, and I know you've been using it for five years or so. I'm not sure if you understand that our application not only makes LogistiNet unnecessary, but is also incompatible with it from a data-exchange standpoint.

Similarly, every element of your gradually developing plan ought to be the subject of a trial balloon at the appropriate time, such as:

○ *I sense your concern about risk. Could we just implement this in one region, as a sort of beta site, without affecting the rest of the company?*

○ *This system would change the way people enter orders pretty substantially. If it resulted in fewer errors long-term, at the cost of some short-term learning-curve issues, would that be the kind of trade-off you're expecting right now?*

○ *A possibility I'm thinking of, to give you more space in the meeting room, is to put your breakfast in the prefunction area. You'll have a lot more space and a change of scenery for your people, but at some sacrifice in privacy during the breakfast period.*

○ *This particular solution will require us to bring all of the managers together for four days of training. Will that be doable if this is the right solution?*

○ *Would you be open to the idea of taking the printing process off-site, if it would cut costs and improve turnaround times?*

Yes, of course you're already doing this—some of the time. The pros do it methodically, all the time. They leave little or nothing to chance. The rest of the world's salespeople manage expectations such as these only when they think they absolutely have to, and then they do it, but they dread it. Most of the time, they leave the bulk of the details unspoken, not contracted, hidden from the prospect's view. Why? I hear reasons such as these:

- *I was so busy...I just didn't get to it all.*

- *It just didn't occur to me that the training, which I was offering completely free of charge, would still look expensive to them, because of travel, hotel stay, time away from the job, and all that.*

- *It would have delayed the proposal. Worse, it might have sent me back to square one, and I couldn't fathom the notion of having to rework the proposal.*

- *I didn't think she really wanted to take another call from me. The last thing she said when I left there was, "I look forward to seeing your proposal next week," so I just figured I shouldn't call.*

- *I was hoping they wouldn't notice or wouldn't care.*

- *I'm pretty fast on my feet. I can usually handle questions and objections really well after they've had a chance to read the proposal.*

You dig into details such as these when you think you absolutely must (and you dread it because you never know what you're going to hear in response), but the *pros* manage every little expectation *not because they think they have to, but because they really want to!* And they don't dread it; they delight in it. Although no salesperson enjoys hearing no, interactive sellers don't fear it. They understand that every big deal they close is the culmination of a journey with a lot of stops and starts, and lots of no and yes responses along the way. They go by the rule *Know Every No*, because the only thing worse than hearing the no is not hearing it.

FROWNS ARE NEARLY AS GOOD AS SMILES

Henry sells managed-care plans to small and midsize employers. He's a pro at floating trial balloons. Henry says a no is very nearly as good as a yes. Here's a story he told me that illustrates the point:

> *I had been working with Suzanne, VP of HR at Spartan Products for about three weeks. The company has around 137 full-time employees in five states. As with most small employers, especially those operating in more than one state, they've had few really attractive options for health insurance. I had some positive momentum going, because we have some brand-new managed-care plans. The company's census and composition seemed a good fit for several plans I could configure. I ran a trial balloon suggesting to Suzanne that we bring their two top executives into the discussions, and that went very well. I don't think any competitor had engaged those guys yet, and I learned that they were partial to a program that gives employees a choice of plans.*
>
> *I started to think about a program I had put together for another prospect, including three options, one of which doesn't even feel like a managed healthcare plan at all. The only limiting factor was state laws in Texas and Massachusetts (two of their five states) preventing one of the options from being included. Fortunately, I found a way to offer a third option in those states that was nearly as good.*

*I floated this trial balloon—I float everything!—
and was surprised to get shut down pretty quickly.
Honestly, the response was out of character for
Suzanne, and not consistent with the optimistic
progress we had been making thus far.*

*I'm sure I had a puzzled look on my face as I asked
Suzanne what the problem was with this approach.
She explained that the Texas division is a separate
corporate entity set up exclusively to supply the par-
ent company. In the past, Spartan had unwittingly
fostered a "poor stepchild" mentality among the
employees, and now goes out of its way to make
sure everything is uniform in all five states. They were
simply not open to entertaining any other approach.*

*I'm glad I hadn't plunged forward with that plan!
This new information sent me in a very different direction. We work with some affiliate companies that
expand the options we can offer, so I was able to
find an affiliate whose plans would pass muster with
every state's regs. Furthermore, this affiliate offers a
very efficient disability plan. So I floated another
trial balloon, this one about disability insurance. And
whaddya know—I just stumbled into another need
that hadn't come up earlier! My value to Spartan
had gone up substantially now that I could supply
options for both managed-care and disability. I got
that deal, and two referrals from their CEO.*

It's okay if the prospect frowns when you float a trial balloon. If the answer was always going to be yes, there'd be no
reason to ask! You can deal with that little no now a lot more
easily than a Big No later. When you encounter a negative reaction to a trial balloon or a half-baked idea, it generates a whole
new batch of questions that help you better understand the
prospect's needs, priorities, capabilities, limitations, flexibility,
decision-making process, and so on. If your first balloon didn't

float, you'll now collect the information you need to ensure that your next balloon will fly. It just might fly as high as Henry's did.

Your Turn

I'm sending you back to your calendar again. Look ahead to the next week or two. Find *three* appointments with important prospects with whom you're beyond the needs-analysis stage, but not really ready to deliver the proposal. Perhaps you're willing and eager to pop the proposal now—you figure you're done selling—but you realize that the prospect isn't finished buying, and you know it would be risky to hand off that proposal. For each of these three midstream situations, list every element that ought to be raised first in trial balloon form.

Managing expectations about price

If you've ever had a prospect nod enthusiastically all the way through your sales presentation and then say no when you reached the end—or three weeks later—quite likely, the reason for the refusal was the price. There are darn few sales in which price is not an issue, and it's often on the short list of determinative issues, but the pros know it often does not sit at the very top of the prospect's list. As a sales executive in the manufacturing field (parts, components, systems) told me, "Of course, we have to compete on price, at some level, but it's not the key thing that drives customers these days. For most companies, there's just no room for error, so consistent quality is their number-one driver, and consistent delivery is a close second." It's not much different in other industries. In sector after sector, price is *almost always* on the list of purchase criteria, but *almost never* at the top. Within any given business category, it's typical to find that the purchase criteria vary from one client to the next. Occasionally, price tops the list, but that's the exception, not the rule.

Discussing price or cost is an expectation-management issue. Knowing when and how to float it is one of the hallmarks of a sales pro. There's one thing of which you can be certain: A prospect who's not privy to price until proposal time isn't truly your partner, *and you are surely not hers.* Perhaps your industry is one in which prices don't vary much from one vendor to the next and are generally known by most of the prospects. But many of you are in fields in which it's all too common to conceal the price until the final page of your proposal, and then to stage what's close to a grand unveiling. When you do unveil it, you communicate nothing if not your trepidation about the commitment you're asking for. You spark thoughts in the prospect that were probably not there before: *Has this guy ever asked for this amount of money before? Is he unsure of the value of what he's offering? Is he wondering how rough the negotiation is going to be? Am I supposed to conclude that the price is highly negotiable? Who calculated this price anyway, this guy or his boss? Should I be talking to the boss?*

Price is almost always on the list, but almost never at the top.

WHEN PRICE COMES ON THE TABLE TOO EARLY

The prospect's budget is another expectation-management issue that salespeople often mishandle, to everyone's detriment. It's routine in many companies that sellers inquire, often at the first meeting with the prospect, what budget has been set aside for this expenditure. Perhaps you work in an industry in which you have little choice, but the vast majority of you do not. Although it's imperative that you talk about price—at the right time—it's often in your best interest *never* to ask about budget. When you do, you disadvantage yourself and your prospect. Here's what happens:

- You put the prospect on guard, raising suspicions that you intend to propose a product or a solution that will drain their budget, even if a smaller investment would have fixed the company's problem quite well, thank you. As a result, most prospects respond with a figure that's more akin to a negotiating position than a true budget number, or they may respond with a lowball figure that's entirely appropriate given their lack of information about the value of your not-yet-developed solution.

- As soon as they trot out that number, you're in a box! Unless you push back and decline to work within that limitation—which you're hardly prepared yet to do—you instantly become limited by the dollar figure the prospect presented to you, whether it's real or not. With that expectation on the table, and no complaint coming from you, you have a contract, a mini-close, long before it's appropriate. Now you'll be out of order if you come back with a proposal that doesn't fit that figure. Oops.

It's better not to know, don't you think? Budgets are real, but that doesn't mean they rule. Each year in America, billions of dollars *budgeted to be spent* never are; and billions more are spent *that were never budgeted*. It's that way in your household, and it's that way in your prospect's company. Rarely does a single expenditure conform to a line-item budget projection. When you aim for a budget number instead of aiming for the best solution with the strongest ROI for your client, you undermine any trust-bond that may have been developing, you fail to deliver the best solution, and you communicate clearly that you're no pro. You've hardly set yourself up for success.

If you've ever been asked upfront—way, way too early in most situations—about the price of your product, you know that's yet another expectation-management challenge many salespeople face. Whatever you say in response sets an expectation, so be careful, and most especially be aware of what you said. Remember it, because I guarantee your prospect will. If he remembers only one thing from his first meeting with you, it was your answer to his question about price.

Whatever you say—or don't say—about price sets an expectation.

There's no single piece of sage advice about how to answer that premature question I can offer that would apply to every reader, representing as you do myriad industries, sectors, segments, and firms. But here are some options, and with each, a translation of the expectation you're communicating:

- In most cases, your best answer—if it's true!—is that pricing is dependent on so many variables, which are in turn dependent on the client's needs and requirements, that it's just not possible to quote a number at this early stage.

  The expectation you just set: You and the prospect will be having detailed discussions about needs and requirements, as well as a broad range of variables. Or stated another way, pricing will itself be an *interactive* process.

- Some sales pros cite a *range* of prices to illustrate and dramatize how dependent pricing is on factors the seller has—at this early stage—no way of knowing: *We've done installations as small as $40,000 and as big as $600,000.*

  The expectations you just set: Similar to the previous example, pricing is dependent on variables, and we have a lot to talk about—plus it's very unlikely that you'll be proposing anything below your low-end figure, or be able to sell anything above your high-end figure. Some prospects press for a narrower range; go ahead and give them one, if you like, but beware of the box you're climbing into.

○ Highballing your answer to that inconvenient question works for some sellers. They cite a high number, and add that they'll "work with" the prospect to make the price digestible.

The expectations you just set: Your final quote will be less than the highball, *and* you're "negotiable."

○ You must answer the question in a plain and candid way, or else...

The expectation you just set: You're sleazy or sketchy.

○ In some industries or with some vendors, it's standard practice to talk about price very early, without even being asked, as a qualification technique. They often express a price range, or mention a minimum figure.

The expectations you've just set: You're not especially interested in business opportunities that fall below your threshold, and you want to know now so you don't waste everyone's time.

○ This conversation about price is *contracting*, of course, so it's probably not inappropriate to pose the reciprocal question to the prospect, but *only after completing your candid answer* to her question. If your answer included specific dollar amounts, it's okay to ask, "Is there a figure that you were expecting to spend?" This is not the same as asking about their budget, because you have not specified "budget," and because you have already gone on record with a price range. You'll be surprised how often the answer is, "No, I didn't have any particular number in mind." If you do hear a figure or a range, it's likely a lowball. If you let that lowball hang there...

The expectation you just set: You'll meet it. If you don't anticipate being able to deliver your product or service at that lowball price, you must say so now.

THE SWEET SPOT

Ideally, questions about price did not arise in the early stage of your interaction with the prospect, or if it did, you were able to postpone the discussion by indicating that there are simply too many variables. Just as your first, and perhaps second, meeting with the prospect is too early for a discussion about dollars—price, unit cost, monthly maintenance, value, whatever—it's equally true that this subject is too important to be held back until the last minute. Understanding that price is often not the driving factor in the prospect's decision, but is instead one element in a matrix of purchase criteria, sales pros deal with it in much the same way they deal with everything else. They trial-balloon it.

Knowing when to float a dollar figure requires finesse. The pros know that sending that balloon up either *too early* or *too late* can damage the process and put the outcome in jeopardy:

> ○ *Too early* is before the prospect has a good handle on how well your solution will meet his needs. Once the prospect's needs have been specifically identified, and the nature of your solution is clear enough to the prospect that he is able to visualize its benefits and its value—and once you have locked down enough variables to be able to run some numbers—it's prime time for your trial balloon on price. Prior to this point, the prospect has no context in which to consider your price, no

benchmark by which to evaluate the dollar figure, so his response to your trial balloon will be
unreliable, and probably unrealistic.

○ *Too late* is any time that's more than a few days
after the prospect has gotten a good handle on
how well your solution will meet his needs. If the
pricing you have in mind for this solution is out
of sync with what the prospect is willing or able
to do, this is information you need to have as
early as possible. Modifying the plan to make it
fit the prospect's parameters—or modifying the
prospect's perception of the value inherent in your
solution—will now become the focus of the re-
mainder of your interactive selling and buying
process.

So yes, there's a sweet spot, a perfect moment to float the
trial balloon about price. The pros keep their antennae tuned
for that moment, and they've prepared themselves in advance
because they're never entirely certain when the sweet spot
will present itself. When they determine the time is right, they
float the balloon in the same low-key, matter-of-fact, underselling manner as every other trial balloon and half-baked
idea. They open the conversation with a phrase similar to this:

○ *I've been playing with some figures I think you
may find workable....*

○ *Some estimates I've come up with look like this....*

○ *I've been thinking about some numbers we might
work with, and here's what I've come up with.
Tell me what you think....*

After you've mentioned your estimate, or your now much
narrower range, wait for the prospect's reaction. A minimal
reaction—or outright consent—requires little further discussion; you just achieved an important mini-close. A less positive
reaction, on the other hand, will prompt a useful conversation—
one that's timely right now, and healthy to have while the

proposal is still a work in progress and modifications are still relatively easy to make. Or perhaps the conversation will be, not about modifying the proposal to make it acceptable to the client company, but about modifying attitudes and expectations within that company about the inherent value of the proposal as it is developing. At this stage, the challenge may be to work on the decision-making process, not the plan you're pro-

Your trial balloon about price will prompt a useful conversation— one that's better to have now than later.

posing. Both you and your prospect are much better off if you're still in the room while those discussions are happening. In other words, if you're using *interactive selling* instead of handoff selling.

But if you've been selling interactively all along, if you've been facilitating the buying process right alongside your selling process, it's a lot less likely that you'll have to deal with a negative reaction to your price estimate. That's one of the many pleasant surprises that greet the salesperson who adopts interactive selling.

Half-baked ideas and trial balloons are your principal tools for ensuring that your proposal is *buyable*—not just saleable. They improve the *proposal* dramatically by integrating the prospect's own contributions, information, ideas, and decisions. And they improve the *prospect* by putting a high percentage of the buying decision into the past, rather than leaving most of it for the day you deliver the proposal.

YOUR TURN

This time I'd like you to look back at your appointments over the last week, or perhaps month…as far back as you need to look to find appointments with *three* prospects who may possibly be ready for a trial balloon about pricing. For each, determine if the sweet spot is here now, by answering these questions:

● Have the prospect's needs, challenges, issues, capabilities, and limitations been identified with sufficient specificity, and agreed upon?

● Have your discussions about the nature of your solution reached the point where your prospect is able to visualize the benefits and the value of the plan that's coming together? Have you seen clear evidence of this?

● Have you locked down enough of the variables that you are able to run some numbers and provide a legitimate estimate, or a narrow range, that's useful and reliable?

If you're saying yes to each question, make arrangements to float a trial balloon about pricing within the next seven days. If you're not certain of the answers, that's the same as a no, in which case your task is to reengage the prospect and reach the sweet spot where it's ideal to float your thoughts about price.

CLOSING THE CHAPTER

I believe these are some of the key takeaways from this chapter:

● Sales pros work transparently, in the sunshine. They know that when all their moves are open, obvious, out there, and *contracted*, they create the depth of trust that leads toward big deals with big customers.

● Their strategy is to seek approval or consent to all the details and to deliver a *no-surprise proposal* every time.

● Half-baked ideas are often about the central concept in your proposed solution, but *trial balloons* are about the important aspects and details of either the *proposed plan* or the *process* leading to it.

○ Any detail you fail to trial-balloon along the way is a potential hazard, and the guiltier you are of *handoff selling*. If the proposal requires a lot of work after it leaves your hands, that work will happen beyond your reach, your input, and your influence.

○ The pros go by the rule *Know Every No*, because the only thing worse than hearing the no is *not* hearing it.

○ Deal with the little no now, rather than face the Big No later.

○ Prospects who are not privy to price until proposal time aren't truly your partners...and you are surely not theirs.

○ Price is a pertinent topic at various stages in the selling cycle, but budget discussions are often misleading, distracting, and risky—for everyone. Each year in America, billions of dollars *budgeted to be spent* never are; and billions more are spent that were *never budgeted.*

○ The *sweet spot* to trial-balloon what your solution might cost arrives as soon as the prospect's needs are specifically identified, *and* the nature of your solution is clear enough to the prospect that he can visualize its value and its benefits.

What are *you* thinking right now, as this chapter closes? What were *your* biggest takeaways? Your feedback is helpful as we continue to build the practices of interactive selling. So please e-mail me now at SteveMarx@InteractiveSelling.com, and put "Chapter 10" in the subject line of your message.

CHAPTER ELEVEN

GET A FASTER ANSWER
WITH A SLOWER PROPOSAL

THERE'S A COMMON MISCONCEPTION IN SELLING THAT THE faster you deliver the proposal, the faster you can get the order. It's rarely true. What's true is this: The faster you deliver the proposal, the faster you *might* get a *decision*. That's a completely different matter. If all you want is a fast decision—*and that's more important than whether it's a yes or a no*—why not just e-mail the proposal and skip the meeting altogether? You'll succeed in looking busy and productive as you churn through prospects, but expect to hear no a lot.

The salespeople I know don't merely want a decision, they want a yes! *Interactive selling* raises your closing percentage and boosts the number of times you hear *yes!* Interactive selling requires you to pay as much attention to the buying process as you already are to the selling process—to stop ne-glecting 50 percent of your job. When you're sell-ing interactively, you make *buying* as much your business as selling is. You make yourself a partner in the buying, and most prospects respond natu-rally by becoming your partner in the selling.

Interactive selling raises your closing percentage.

Interactive salespeople never lose their focus, not just on the prospect, but on the buying process itself. They break down the mountain of doubt, the complexities and multiple depen-dencies inherent in so many buying decisions today, turning them into incremental, logical, consecutive, *molehill decisions.* In so doing, they literally make buying easier for the prospect— perhaps the ultimate definition of the salesperson's job.

Your check-valve in a long selling cycle

The pros constantly track the decision-making process, aware at all times of which pieces and parts of the not-yet-delivered proposal are already "bought" and by whom—and which still remain to be decided, to be closed. As selling cycles get longer and the number of decision-makers and decision-influencers increases, tracking the buying process becomes more complex, and the risks go up. You know from your own experience how common it's becoming that the cast of charac-ters changes before the deal is done, and how much more likely it is now that unexpected events will arise that are hazardous to your sale.

Progress reports—some sales pros call them *pre-proposals* or *partial proposals*—are a valuable tool for interactive sell-ers when helping to manage a complex buying process, espe-cially one that happens in slow-motion. Unlike *homework assignments, half-baked ideas,* and *trial balloons,* which are verbal and can appear to be spontaneous, progress reports are always written documents. Their purpose is to document the progress that's been made up to that point, to specify what's already been agreed to, to focus on a shorter list of items yet to be determined, to lock in what's been accomplished, and to provide a platform and a path for what's yet to be done—by gaining the prospect's "so far, so good" approval.

Progress reports help "lock in" portions of a complex sale, so the parties can focus forward.

Think of the progress report as a kind of "check-valve," designed to keep decisions from flowing backward through the decision pipeline, to ensure that decisions previously made remain made. They help facilitate the next steps by gaining the prospect's consent or approval for the concepts and details, the pieces and parts, to which they've already nodded their agreement—key elements you anticipate will be in your final proposal. These formal progress reports require a response from the client, and in return, they offer a variety of benefits to both buyer and seller. Among other things, they:

- Enhance the prospect's engagement and support by transitioning from their informal approval of a series of verbally presented elements, to their more formal agreement with a written summation of these same elements.

- Help uncover problems, such as misunderstandings and other gaps and gulches, which you may not have realized exist.

- Deflect your competitors, by holding the attention and delaying the decision of the prospect.

- Give your prospect something to share with other decision-influencers in the organization, people you may not have the opportunity to interface with, to keep them apprised of your work together, to build support, and to secure their approval.

Jim is a sales pro with LogistiCo, a logistics and warehousing contractor. Here's an example of how Jim uses progress reports:

Mitch, the new senior VP of operations at BlueStar Medicorp, was eager to find a replacement for the warehousing, logistics, and delivery supplier the company had long used. Jim was already about six weeks deep into the selling-and-buying process with Mitch, and sensed things were going well, when Mitch casually mentioned that he was so optimistic about LogistiCo's ability to meet BlueStar's needs that he was now going to bring two of his key people, Cheryl and Ted, into the loop on this project, people who had been at BlueStar much longer than Mitch had.

The wheels started not just turning, but spinning inside Jim's head. He didn't know Cheryl and Ted; he should and would suggest a meeting in which he could get their input and engagement. But he had no idea when they'd be able to schedule that meeting, so he responded to Mitch by saying, "I'd love to meet them and get their input. In the meantime, I'd like to document for you the progress we've made over these last six weeks, put it in writing, so as to make it easier for you to describe to Cheryl and Ted just what we've been talking about." Jim's strategy here was to be "in the room" even when he wasn't in the room. Mitch responded, "That'd be terrific. Really helpful. Thank you."

Back at the office, Jim crafted a progress report that was simple and straightforward. It was three pages long. The first page detailed BlueStar's needs as Mitch and Jim had determined them, the second page gave the framework of LogistiCo's plan to remedy the problems with the existing logistics firm and provide superior service, and on the third page, Jim listed as many open issues and unresolved details as he could. By delivering a document with a significant list of open items, Jim hoped that neither Cheryl nor Ted would view Mitch's plan as a fait accompli hatched without their involvement, but would instead see substantial opportunities for them to have input and impact. The same strategy had worked the previous month with Community Newspapers. Jim's notes were pretty good, so it only took him 45 minutes to put this progress report together. He e-mailed it to Mitch before the close of business.

Mitch called a week later to tell Jim how very impressed both Ted and Cheryl were, and how much they were looking forward to meeting Jim and fine-tuning the LogistiCo plan.

WHEN A PROGRESS REPORT MIGHT BE WISE

Jim's success using a progress report with BlueStar suggests one of the situations in which a progress report is helpful—not only to the salesperson, but to the prospect as well. Here's a longer list. Consider which of the following circumstances occur in the type of selling you do and whether or not a progress report would be helpful:

- When there's a substantial amount of information on the table, and you need a way to clarify, document, or organize it for the benefit of your staff or the client's.

- When you want to nail down informal or verbal agreements on a concept or a direction, and move on to a discussion of details and/or implementation.

- When you want to present two or more distinct alternatives, and they're too intricate to be described verbally.

- When there are new or additional decision-makers or decision-influencers who need to be brought up-to-date or into the loop, or when some key people are distantly located and you're unable to meet with them.

- When you have a prospect whose consent might not be reliable until he's seen the pertinent information in writing.

- When you believe you need to maintain credibility and a competitive edge in the midst of a lengthy selling cycle.

Formal progress reports, along with homework assignments, half-baked ideas, and trial balloons, help move the purchase and sale forward in increments. Each is contracting in its purest form, each works to integrate the buying process into the selling process, and each can help you close like the pros.

YOUR TURN

Look back now at the six prospects you selected for the two Your Turn personal workshops in Chapter 10. Select the three that are the most complex sales you have pending—complex either because of the nature of the solution you're proposing, or because of the number of decision-influencers who will have a chance to stir the broth. Run each of the three projects you selected past the six situations on the list of when you should use a progress report. Determine which ones, if any, would benefit by your circulating a written progress report before making your final recommendations. For each prospect you think should get a progress report, at what point should it be distributed?

CRITICAL PATH: HOW THE PROS' PROPOSALS DIFFER FROM THE REST

Contracting—and mini-closing—never ends. The pros do it, not as often as *necessary*, but as often as *possible*. For them it continues right into the day they finally deliver their no-surprise proposal and expect the order, and it carries on beyond that day, for as long as that client remains a client.

Your sales proposal is already quite good, if it meets these three tests:

- ○ It specifies the prospect's needs.
- ○ It clearly describes your tailored solution to those needs.
- ○ It contains no surprises.

Now I want you to add one more element—it's more contracting!—that you may not have in your proposals right now. It's your final mini-close. It's called the *critical path*, and it's the final page of your proposal.

The critical path is a list of key actions along the path to success in meeting the client's need or solving his problem. It's half history and half projection. The *history* portion is roughly the top half of your critical path page, tracing the dates and events that brought you and the prospect to this point. It's a gentle reminder to the prospect of how much of a partner she has been and how much contribution she has made to the proposal. The *projection* portion is the bottom half of the page, laying out all the steps that must be taken by each party to ensure that the client's needs are fully met and the solution yields the maximum value possible. It assures the prospect of flawless execution and outstanding customer care, beginning the moment she gives the go-ahead. It's a to-do list for everybody, and when it sits there as your final page, it makes a much

> *The critical path is half history and half projection.*

better subject for discussion and fine-tuning than if you were to devote your last page to what most salespeople do: the grand unveiling of the total cost.

Here's an example of a critical path Barbara used to close a proposal for her management recruiting firm to find 40 metro area managers for a quick-service restaurant chain that was scaling up rapidly:

DATE	ACTION TAKEN/TO BE TAKEN	BY WHOM
28 Nov 06	Initial meeting	JS, BL
12 Dec 06	Discussion/demonstration of capabilities and resources	JS, BL
9 Jan 07	Comprehensive needs analysis	JS, GF, BL
10 Jan 07	Follow-up needs analysis (teleconference)	JS, BL
18 Jan 07	Review of basic concept and research plan; funding confirmed	JS, GF, BL
7 Feb 07	Interviews of 20 high-performing managers completed	BL, AS, RP
13 Feb 07	Data analysis presentation re high performers	JS, BL, AS
1 Mar 07	Additional data presentation for CEO	JC, JS, BL
6 Mar 07	Brainstorming session re recruitment sources	GF, BL, etc.
7 Mar 07	Conference with in-house legal counsel	JS, LH, BL
15 Mar 07	Final recommendations	JS, GF, BL
20 Mar 07	Project teams assembled	JS, BL
26 Mar 07	Beta testing of telephone screener questionnaire completed	BL, MC
28 Mar 07	Advertising program developed and placed	BL, CJ
28 Mar 07	Outbound calls begin to candidates on internal list	BL, MC
1 Apr 07	Inbound calls begin to 24-hour recruitment center	BL, team
9 Apr 07	First-week metrics report	JS, BL, AS
11 Apr 07	Second-stage telephone screening for top 20% begins	BL, MC
23 Apr 07	Invitations to top 5% to travel to Indianapolis assessment center	JS, BL, TM
31 May 07	Referral of finalist candidates	BL

As you can see in Barbara's example, the date of the proposal itself (15 March 2007) should appear about halfway down the page, so approximately half is *history* and half is *projection*. Barbara's critical path sends a strong message to her prospect that he will get as much attention and support *after* he says yes as he got before—and what a breath of fresh air that is in a world suffering from too many *love 'em and leave 'em* salespeople.

Chris, who sells Internet advertising and marketing solutions, told me:

I don't fancy myself a hard closer. That stuff would embarrass me and I've seen it alienate prospects. And I don't need it! Closing is easier for both of us if I've been contracting and mini-closing from the outset. Then the critical path is just the last piece of this strategy. For me, it has replaced those awkward closing questions. You know, "Have I earned your business?" or, "So, are you ready for the pen?" or, "Shall I have my office input this order?" Eeeww!

I use the critical path every time. My clients have gotten so used to me contracting the next steps— we've done it so often before—and they've seen that I'm 100 percent reliable and do exactly what I said I would do...that contracting the next steps as they appear on the critical path just feels natural to them. And to me too.

I don't think someone who's not an interactive seller can just drop a critical path onto the back of all their proposals and expect it to work wonders, but if you've been contracting all along and your proposal doesn't contain any curveballs, it's downright amazing how well it works. I'm delivering fewer proposals—but writing way more business— now. Oh, and the critical path doesn't just help me close the business. It really is the critical path we all

follow—everyone at my company and at the clients'—
to implement the solution. Client satisfaction and
retention are up as a direct result.

To put the spotlight on contracting the next steps (that is, the steps involved in implementing the plan you just sold), position the critical path as the final page of your no-surprise proposal or progress report. No longer will the final page be reserved for the price quote, because the price tag was successfully trial-ballooned previously and is now just one more nonsurprise. It appears somewhere in the body of the proposal, as one of the many parameters, details, and specifications. A proposal that concludes with the critical path is far stronger than one that ends with the price. The last page provides the image that lingers—quite literally—in the mind of the client, and inevitably dominates the conversation that follows the formal delivery of the proposal. When you use the critical path and place it at the end, the lingering image will be a review of the prospect's investment in and contribution to the proposal and a projection of plan implementation and customer care.

YOUR TURN

Although you would not want to start building a critical path for every prospect as soon as you meet him, neither do you want to wait until the evening before your presentation to start pulling all the information together. Somewhere between your first meeting and your final one, once you sense this deal may be going in a very good direction, start assembling the critical path in an electronic file you can keep editing along the way. Good record-keeping habits will make it much easier to reconstruct dates and events back to the beginning of the selling cycle. Even before you deliver the critical path, that online document will help *you* stay focused on the next steps.

Now choose the two most important proposals you're working on at this time. Review your notes and your day-planner or online calendar, and begin building, for each of these prospects, the critical path you'll place at the end of the no-surprise proposal when you present it. If it's tough to reconstruct the history, adopt some new habits and systems that will leave you with a more comprehensive paper trail for future proposals.

THE TORTOISE'S PROPOSAL

Interactive sellers who define their job as helping to facilitate the buying process *delay delivery* of their proposal until they believe the yes decision is ready. They understand that the presentation of their final recommendations is similar to passing that baton in a relay race. They know that as soon as they pass the proposal, they may as well head to the showers, and periodically check the scoreboard to see how they did. Like a pro ballplayer, they don't want that shower until the game is over. So they have trial-ballooned everything, obtained consent for every aspect of the plan from every decision-influencer, or as one sales pro said to me, "They're begging for the proposal by the time I deliver it."

Integrating buying into selling and making them into one seamless, mutually supportive process, is just the opposite of what most salespeople do. Most are in a hurry—they seem to be chasing an answer, instead of pursuing a yes. They use their first appointment to gather information. Then, they head back to the office to work on the proposal, perhaps conferring with a sales manager, product engineer, or applications specialist to get feedback on an idea or on the proposal itself. But rarely do they check with the person who can *really* offer valuable, proposal-developing information: *the prospect.* They complete the proposal as

> *The moment you deliver the proposal, you may as well head to the showers.*

quickly as possible, believing (as they've been taught) that the sooner they put it in the prospect's hands, the sooner they'll have their order. What they hear instead is, "Give me some time to think about it"—followed by a trip to the shower.

They're on the phone a few days later, cooking up reasons to call when there's really nothing more to add to the very comprehensive proposal they left behind. Their only option is to wait, patiently or impatiently, while the prospect compares their proposal to others on the table, checks with people in his firm, investigates the details, crunches the numbers, and troubleshoots the problem areas. Or does nothing at all. And eventually, the decision comes down...or the total absence of communication from the prospect helps the hapless salesperson come to the only logical conclusion. He didn't place any numbers on the scoreboard that day.

That's *handoff selling*...the most common form of selling in the world today, in spite of the fact that it fails so often. It's handoff selling when the buying process doesn't begin until the selling process has concluded and the proposal is handed off. The buyer has little or no involvement in the selling process, and the seller has little or no involvement in the buying process. The buyer's help and the buyer's ideas are absent while the proposal is being developed, and the seller's ideas and the seller's help are missing while the proposal is being evaluated. Selling and buying happen *sequentially*.

Handoff Selling

Interactive Selling

Interactive selling stands in sharp contrast. Here, the proposal is an ever-present work in progress, an iterative process that:

- Begins to take shape almost immediately after the seller and buyer begin working together.

- Is present in one form or another at every stage of the process.

- Goes through informal rough draft after informal rough draft, nursed along with homework assignments, half-baked ideas, trial balloons, and the occasional progress report.

- Is slaved over nearly as much by the buyer as by the seller.

By the time the proposal generated by an interactive selling and buying process is completed and put on paper, it holds no surprises and is nearly a done-deal. Selling and buying happen *simultaneously*.

When you slooowww down the proposal by involving the prospect in its creation, you actually *speed up* the decision-making process. Instead of happening in tandem, they happen together. As important a member of the "proposal development team" as you are, the prospect contributes his thoughts—and shoots down some of yours—throughout the idea-generating, problem-solving, solution-polishing, detail-crunching, proposal-developing process. By the time the proposal is ready, *so is the yes*.

Slowing down the proposal often speeds up the decision-making process.

Timothy sells commercial/industrial cleaning services. Here's what he learned about cranking out proposals:

> *My manager was always pushing me to get more proposals out there. In fact, at one point, we had a contest going in the department to see who could get the most proposals pumped out in a month. I won. I got a nice trip to the Bahamas. But in reality,*

I lost. It was one of my worst months from a revenue standpoint, trip or no trip.

I went back and counted the number of follow-up calls I made after those 17 proposals. I made 67 what I call "have you come to a decision yet?" calls. Oh, I was busy, but my closing ratio went down the tubes. All but one of those 17 prospects asked for time to think about what I had proposed, and most never bought anything.

I've got a new manager now who gets it. I'm doing less than eight proposals a month, but selling 40 percent more. I won't even deliver a proposal to prospects until they have had input on the solution, the details, the expected results, the implementation, and definitely the price. This is the only way to work!

Marian sells metal components and products used mostly in construction. She knows how to put the odds in her favor:

Have you ever heard of the magic proposal? That's what I call my proposals these days. Magic proposals are ones I don't have to develop by myself.

Let me give you an example. I was working with a home builder who was in the planning stages of a new development. They had put out an RFP for 200 streetlight poles. Their architect had already specified the size and type of unit they were looking for, so my technical people could help me spec this thing out pretty easily. But I knew who some of the other bidders were, and we can almost never match their prices.

Instead of just submitting a proposal, I decided to scope out the site a bit and learn more about the development. I called the developer who referred me to Ed, the design engineer who was working with the architectural firm. When it became clear I had done my homework and knew something about the development, the project planner agreed to meet with me to talk about a few ideas I had rolling around in my head.

Frankly, he didn't care for most of my ideas, but one of them piqued his interest in a big way. We had a particular style of light pole that was outside of their specs, but fit in perfectly with the look they were trying to achieve in the community. The planner started getting excited. Of course, reality set in and the developer wasn't willing to increase his budget for street lighting. So we put our heads together—the project planner and I—and we worked out a design that used fewer poles and different lamps. It actually provided more lumens on every block and really contributed to the look and feel the project team had in mind from the beginning. By the time they got that proposal, my order was pretty much in the bag, because it was as much their proposal as mine. That's what I call a magic proposal! I could tell you more stories....

With interactive selling, the buying process begins as soon as the selling process does, and the selling process continues until the buying process is completed. Indeed, the two are so interwoven that a fly on the wall would have a hard time telling which activities are selling and which are buying. Interactive selling also:

- Maintains the prospect's interest and optimism while the proposal is under development.
- Lessens the burden on you to develop the "perfect solution" all by yourself.
- Weeds out—nice and early—those concepts and solutions the prospect can't or won't buy.

⚬ Saves you the precious time and resources lost on ultimately futile proposals—time you can invest in better opportunities.

When you integrate and synchronize selling and buying, everyone benefits. *You and the prospect create a better proposal* (one more likely to be bought, and one more likely to result in customer satisfaction and repeat purchases), and *you and the proposal create a better prospect* (one more engaged, more invested, more comfortable, more likely to buy, and more likely to be satisfied).

As with the proverbial tortoise and hare, the slooowww proposal has the better chance of winning the race.

CLOSING THE CHAPTER

I believe these are some of the key takeaways from this chapter:

⚬ It's a common misconception that the faster you deliver the proposal, the faster you can get the order.

⚬ Aim not for a *fast* decision, but for a *yes* decision.

⚬ Use *progress reports* to place a "check-valve" into a lengthy selling cycle, to keep decisions from flowing backward through the decision pipeline, to lock in the progress you've made, and to build a foundation for moving forward to the sale.

⚬ Use a *critical path* as the last page of your formal proposal. It lists the steps along the path toward your win-win outcome—half *history* and half *projection*.

⚬ The critical path sets up the last of the prospect's *molehill decisions*, and assures her of your continuing care, attention, guidance, and support after she says yes.

- ◐ The day you deliver your formal proposal is *the day you remove yourself from the buying process.* That's why the pros hold the proposal back until they believe the decision is ready.

- ◐ The tortoise reminds us that the slooowwww proposal has the better chance of winning the race.

Let's stay interactive, okay? I'd really like to know your thoughts, your concerns, and your questions as you conclude this chapter. It's easy to e-mail me at SteveMarx@InteractiveSelling.com, and it's very helpful if you write "Chapter 11" in the subject line before you hit Send.

CHAPTER TWELVE

PAYOFF: YOUR POST-SALE PARTNER

NOT ALL OF YOUR CLIENTS AND PROSPECTS ARE SALESPEOPLE. But every one of us in sales is a client—someone's customer—almost every day. When you're the client, which kind of salesperson do you prefer to deal with? The *hyperactive bulldozer* who puts you through his paces and leaves you feeling hustled, the *reactive gofer* who offers little real help and leaves you feeling very alone with your decision, or the *interactive partner* who works at your side to develop and tailor the best solution? Would you choose the seller who helps you buy, or the one whose focus is on nailing his sale?

I've known *no one* who wants to be called on by a bulldozer. There's a smattering of folks who occasionally like being indulged by a submissive gofer, and a few find it easier to deal with a gofer because they know more about what the guy is selling than he does. But fully 95 percent of us would choose the *interactive seller* every time. Your prospects are no different; in fact, millions of prospects out there are waiting for a helpful, creative, interactive partner to walk through the door. They're looking for a salesperson who doesn't jabber on about "partnership," but who *functions* as their partner in every way. They're eager to throw their business the interactive partner's way.

That's why we've said this is one of the few books ever published about selling that you could actually share with your clients and prospects! There are no gambits and no ploys, no trick and no traps, in interactive selling. There's nothing here you would not proudly share with every client, every prospect, every acquaintance, with your mom and dad, your impressionable youngsters, and your revered pastor. Every practice of interactive selling is *deliberately transparent*. Openness, transparency, and shared control over the pace and direction of the integrated selling and buying process is at the very core of how the interactive seller does business. By breaking the mountain down into molehills, buying is made easier, and the process is made more pleasant and productive. If you're an interactive salesperson, *you can shout it from the rooftops!*

You can share this book with your pastor!

When a hyperactive salesperson is on the scene, prospects feel *controlled* and *sold*. When a reactive salesperson is on their account, they feel *neglected* and *nervous*. But when they have the pleasure of dealing with an interactive salesperson, prospects feel *trusted* and *trusting*. I know; they've told me. Here's a longer list of adjectives I've heard from your clients over the years:

With a **hyperactive salesperson,** *the prospect feels...*	*With a* **reactive salesperson,** *the prospect feels...*	*With an* **interactive salesperson,** *the prospect feels...*
Controlled	Neglected	Engaged
Manipulated	Uninformed	Involved
Ignored	Obeyed	Heard
Hustled	Confused	Respected
Processed	Perplexed	Empowered
Pressured	Bewildered	Appreciated
Rushed	Worried	Helped
Abused	Hesitant	Trusted
Sold	Nervous	Trusting

What's especially interesting is that so many hyperactive salespeople are *not* abusive, don't think of themselves as high-pressure, and certainly don't mean to hustle anyone, and yet too often they leave their prospects—whether closed or not—with those very feelings. It's the bulldozer's basic modus operandi that gets her in trouble, that engenders feelings in the prospect of being processed, manipulated, and controlled. Her mode is to focus on the sale instead of the purchase, to take the prospect through the prescribed steps in a cookie-cutter way, to move at a pace and in a direction that's good for the seller without ever getting in sync with the buyer. Even the nicest, most charming hyperactive salesperson—as many of you are—prompts *distance* and *resistance* in his prospects, just by continuing his outdated approach.

YOUR PRE-SALE PARTNER BECOMES YOUR POST-SALE PARTNER

When you conduct yourself as a partner prior to the sale, you'll be seen as one after the sale. When you turn your prospect into a partner before the deal is even done, he'll remain so long after. This is the long-term payoff of interactive selling, the oh-so-sweet fruit of your upfront labor, the outsized return on your savvy investment of time, attention, care, and resources. The bulldozers and gofers of the sales trade can only dream about having a portfolio of clients as fabulous, as forthcoming, and as forgiving as those of the interactive partner.

The post-sale partner is the outsized return on your savvy investment of time, attention, care, and resources.

Here's a look at life with *post-sale partners*:

They're much more likely to be satisfied clients. Perhaps even super-satisfied clients. Your interactive process produced a solution far more tailored to their needs than would otherwise have been possible. Their input, information, and ideas made the plan measurably better in every respect. Buyer's remorse is unknown in the world of interactive selling, and the hassle of dealing with a defective or deficient system, service, or installation is a very rare occurrence.

They welcome and appreciate your continuing involvement. Your ongoing attention to whether the clients' expectations are being met by your product, service, or system is greatly appreciated, because they don't doubt your intent. They know you wear your agenda on your sleeve, that you're truly interested in monitoring their satisfaction with their purchase, that you want to ensure that value is being delivered, and that you won't be coy or devious if you see an opportunity to make another sale that will be of mutual benefit.

They quickly come to consider you a preferred vendor. That preference may be an informal, even unstated, designation, but more and more firms are formalizing their program of preferred-vendor status. They're narrowing the number of suppliers they deal with, and enhancing their relationship with those who are left—in many cases, they're initiating the interactive partnership with vendors who respond. Preferred suppliers are given greater access to the company's people, data, and information; they're called in earlier than other bidders; and they enjoy the benefit of the doubt based on their proven prior performance.

They call you first when they need help. Every salesperson's dream is to have the "first-mover advantage." Proven partners are top of mind with clients, so they get the call asking for help or consultation very early, often before there is even any clarity about the need or problem, let alone the solution sought. When you're the first vendor on the case, you help frame the issues, the process, and the parameters of the solution. You'll ensure the client wins as you ensure you win.

They're less likely to force you to compete on price alone. Clients of the interactive seller come to know instinctively that the measure of value is far more complex and nuanced than mere price per item, per pound, or per month. The interactive process yields a superior solution that's valued in myriad ways (think back to Chapter 11 and the story of Marian's streetlight poles, with better lighting and better-looking poles). If you're a genuine partner, your clients want the benefit of your continued input and problem-solving, and they won't risk that relationship with a tussle over a few percentage points one way or the other.

They know the measure of value is not found merely in the price per item, per pound, or per month.

They have a new benchmark for good sales process. After experiencing a truly professional, highly interactive partnership, your clients' expectations are forever raised. No longer will they tolerate, or talk themselves into the adequacy of, the hyperactive or reactive salesperson. Those who don't practice interactive selling are permanently disadvantaged.

They become a steady source of referrals and recommendations. Clients are thrilled when they find good help, whether that's someone they hire for their staff, or a salesperson who becomes part of their "adjunct staff." They'll talk you up to colleagues both inside and outside their company, and they'll make referrals and introductions without a second thought.

They'll gladly provide you with a testimonial. You already know that testimonials from satisfied clients are among the strongest door-openers you could ever have. Because you sold interactively, you produced a better solution for your clients. Their delight with both your process and your solution will make them much more likely to provide the kind of impressive testimonial that opens eyes and doors.

You'll like your job better. As your client list evolves into one filled with post-sale partners, you'll experience less client turnover and suffer less personal burnout...and you'll enjoy more self-actualization and make more money.

WHEN SOMETHING GOES WRONG

You've already figured out there's yet another benefit to having a post-sale partner. Yes, sooner or later, something will go wrong with some of your clients, despite all the care and ongoing contracting you use. It happens in a marriage, among friends, in the workplace, and of course, between a vendor and a customer. When something gets sideways, you'll especially appreciate that you've got a post-sale partner.

Tensions can ratchet up fast, and in today's typical vendor-client relationships, they often reach the boiling point. When the salesperson has been *hyperactive*, by determining the client's need and devising the answer in an independent fashion, the prospect typically feels as though he is *not accountable* for the project, its functionality, or its ROI. He dumps it in the seller's lap and demands a remedy. The hyperactive seller often will enable this one-way accountability. This is especially true at the growing legion of "superior customer service" companies. At these companies, the mindset too often is either to treat the customer as a small child—whose every whim and quirk is to be indulged, lest we upset her—or to make the process totally turnkey, the you-won't-have-to-lift-a-finger school of sales and marketing. The customer is accountable only to the extent that he has to show up for appointments and meet payment terms; beyond that, it's the vendor who is accountable for *everything* else.

That kind of one-way accountability is okay—until something goes wrong. Then customers start waving your warranty and remembering your every representation. They become emotional, demanding, and threatening. "I want my money back," they say. "I'll take my business elsewhere, and I'll tell all my friends to do the same." Or, "I'm calling my lawyer!"

If the client made his purchase from a *reactive* salesperson, the story may be much the same, though I've seen these clients feel *solely accountable* for the pickle they're in, as all the decisions were theirs, not the gofer's.

Interactive sellers, in contrast, find that times of trouble become an opportunity for collaboration, not an occasion for conflict. Because partners share not only control and decision-making but accountability as well, the prospect is likely to feel *mutually accountable* with the seller for whatever situation has developed. Let's look at an example that dramatizes the difference between a *hyperactive* and an *interactive* salesperson:

When Gwen arrived for work Monday morning at Shoreside Conference Center, she knew she was in for a long day; maybe a long week. The service employees union had set up a picket line, and although they didn't interfere with her reaching her office, she knew the Center would be operating with a skeleton staff and unable to run the events that were booked until the strike was resolved. Topmost in her mind was the annual awards banquet of the Certified Life Under-writers, scheduled for that evening in the Grandview Room. There were to be 200 guests, including spouses.

After confirming with her boss that the event could not go forward at Shoreside, Gwen got to work right away on finding an alternate facility. She called everyone she knew in the business. Rooms big enough for dinner for 200, including a head table and multimedia facilities, weren't all that plentiful on even three months' notice, and Gwen had but hours. Miraculously, in 35 minutes she struck paydirt at the Regal Hotel downtown. She e-mailed her event orders to the Regal's banquet manager, so preparations could begin there. Feeling somewhat victorious, she called Rhonda, her contact with the CLU group.

"What do you mean we can't have the banquet at Shoreside?" Rhonda screamed into the phone. She hadn't enjoyed much about her dealings with Gwen, who always seemed to think her ideas were better than Rhonda's. And she didn't really trust Gwen, though she couldn't put her finger on the reason why. "Did you know this was coming? How long have you known about this? Why didn't you call me last week?" No amount of denials could convince Rhonda that Gwen was blindsided by this. Finally, Gwen was able to tell Rhonda about the Regal, figuring that would calm her down. It didn't.

Rhonda proceeded to rattle off her reasons. "The invitations say 'sunset on the deck' at Shoreside. The award plaques are engraved with the date and the location—they all say Shoreside." Gwen tried to bring the conversation back to more urgent subjects. "Rhonda, let's get started calling the guests and letting them know to go to the Regal tonight." But Rhonda wasn't done sounding off. "And the Regal gets $12 for parking and always has a long line at the valet stand. One reason we chose Shoreside was all your free parking. I can't believe you're doing this to the CLUs. How long have you known about this?"

Again, Gwen tried to bring the conversation around to notifying guests of the new location. "Rhonda, I would be more than happy to help you make calls. E-mail me the list of phone numbers and I will personally get started right now." Gwen hoped her willingness to make calls would show her concern, but it only brought another outburst. "I can't give you the CLUs' phone numbers! What are you thinking? We have standards of privacy to maintain. What would they say to me if they knew you people had gotten hold of their phone numbers?"

Larry sits in the cubicle next to Gwen. He too is a Shoreside sales rep. He could tell that Gwen was getting the third degree again this morning. He thought to himself that this happens to Gwen a lot more than it happens to him. Larry had driven through the picket line about 15 minutes before Gwen, and his situation was even more urgent than hers. Larry had the Grandview Room booked for lunch today! It was the volunteer thank-you luncheon for the Medical Center Women's Guild. They were expecting 175 people.

The first thing Larry did was think of some alternatives and jot down some notes. Then he picked up the phone, not to call the first possibility on his list, but to call Ann, the Guild's luncheon chair. "I feel really bad about this, Ann, but I have some ideas to run by you, different ways of solving our problem and I need to know which one you want me to work on first." He then proceeded to mention four alternatives: postponing the luncheon to a later date; finding a hotel that could handle the group on short notice; seeing if Dino's Restaurant directly across the lake could handle it, because it's large enough and they're closed on Mondays, though they might not be able to call in enough staff quickly enough; and lastly, a really off-the-wall idea. "Are you ready for this? You'll probably ask me what I'm smoking, but here goes. You know the Cherry Festival is in full swing at the fairgrounds. A friend of mine has a huge tent right along the midway that seats at least 250, and he does events at night. They're never booked at noon. I think I can get him to open up. For less than you would have spent with us, we can get free admission, lots of festival food—I know it's not fancy, but it's fun—and the women can enjoy the Cherry Festival all afternoon if they wish."

Larry was ready to jump into action and pursue whichever possibility felt best to Ann. He hoped she'd go for the festival idea, because it was easier—and she did! "Larry, you're always so full of ideas. Maybe all the work we did together on this year's volunteer luncheon, we can just figure that will be the plan for next year! And when life hands you lemons, you make lemonade. So Larry, see if you can do the Cherry Festival and make sure there are pitchers of lemonade on every table. I'll stand up and make a bit out of it."

Larry still had a busy morning making this change happen in the next two hours and 25 minutes, but he was charged up. Larry has terrific clients who make the job fun and fulfilling.

Let's be clear. Larry has terrific clients because *he makes them so*. They act as partners, not pugilists, because of the way Larry interacts with them. Because Larry gets his clients fully engaged in the process, actively involved in producing the plan, and fully invested in it, his clients aren't prone to finger-pointing. Instead, they approach problems with a desire to inquire, to understand, to troubleshoot, and to work alongside him to fix whatever needs to be fixed and improve whatever needs to be improved. If you think Ann is just a sweetie and Larry is just lucky, here's the backstory. Ann used to book some events at the Biltmore back when Gwen was in banquet sales there, and *Gwen had a lot of trouble with Ann*. When Ann first phoned Shoreside, the sales rep she was assigned to was Gwen, but she asked to be reassigned.

You know the old story about the three umpires discussing how they call balls and strikes. The first ump says, "I call 'em as I see 'em." The second one says, "I call 'em as they are!" The third umpire says, "They ain't nuthin 'til I call 'em." To a greater extent than you want to believe, your clients ain't nuthin 'til you make 'em—engaged or alienated, easy or tough, opponents or partners.

When something goes wrong, you really discover how superb a partner you've been. You'll find that challenges are tackled by the partnership *as a team*, not by you alone. Clients know you, your values, your process, and your intentions better from having already worked with you, and they'll stay seated next to you—not across from you— to put things back on track. Being a true interactive partner protects business relationships when a mistake is made, just as surely as it protects our personal relationships when they come under stress.

Interactive partners have a thick layer of protection when something goes wrong.

Even when everything seems to be going right, your partnership needs constant attention and maintenance. Friendships and marriages don't remain strong if the effort that went into creating them is allowed to wither and fizzle. And so it is in sales. Every one of your current clients is your prospect too. And they're also your competitors' prospects. Interactive selling must continue to be your strategy for as long as you work with that client. Don't let a competitor get a foothold by letting your interactive business relationship atrophy and fade into a sloppy or routine hyperactive or reactive one.

YOUR PROSPECTS *will* FIND
THEIR PARTNERS

Prospects prefer partners—interactive salespeople—because the experience is more pleasant, more productive, more profitable, and more perpetuating than it is with mere vendors. And they *will* find their partners, just as Ann did when she rejected Gwen and chose to work with Larry. Whether the partner your prospects find is *you* or *someone else*...that's your decision.

If you want to close like the pros, then make partnership your *path*, not merely your destination.

The very next time you approach a prospect to set up your initial appointment, make sure it's going to be an effective appointment by using *contracting* to address and align expectations in advance. Jump-start the buying process as you're initiating the selling process, from your very first contact. The next time you visit an existing client with whom you hope to build your volume, have some *half-baked ideas* ready that respond to their needs. Don't leave that appointment without making *homework assignments*. Break the natural mountain of doubt down into *incremental molehills* of decision. *Trial-balloon everything* and decide to deliver only *no-surprise proposals*. And never stop contracting, never stop *managing expectations*, before and during every client meeting.

Have your competitors read *Close Like the Pros?* If you're still not sure about the value interactive selling can have for you, answer this question for yourself: *Would you want to be in a competitive battle for a prospect's business—or an existing client's continued business—if you knew your competitor was helping his prospect with each step of the buying decision and you were just focused on your sale, if you knew that your competitor was using interactive selling and you were not?*

With interactive selling:
You and the prospect create a better proposal, while you and the proposal create a better prospect.

CLOSING THE CHAPTER

I believe these are some of the key takeaways from this chapter:

- There are no gambits and no ploys, no tricks and no traps, in *interactive selling*. Every practice of interactive selling is *deliberately transparent*.

- Many hyperactive salespeople are among the nicest, most charming people you'll meet, and they certainly do not mean to abuse their clients—nonetheless they prompt *distance* and *resistance* in their prospects.

- The partner you create before the sale becomes the post-sale partner you are fortunate to have for years to come.

- The bulldozers and gofers out there can only dream about having a portfolio of clients as fabulous, forthcoming, and forgiving as those of the *interactive seller*.

- Eventually, something gets sideways in every business relationship. For interactive sellers, such times of trouble are an opportunity for collaboration, not an occasion for conflict.

- Would you want to be in a tough battle for a big piece of business if you knew your competitor was using *interactive selling* and you were not?

- This may be the first book about selling that you'd feel comfortable sharing with your clients and prospects.

Now that you've finished the entire book, I'm especially eager to know what the big takeaways have been for *you*. Please e-mail me at SteveMarx@InteractiveSelling.com, and be sure to put "Chapter 12" in the subject line so I'll know you've finished the book.

INDEX

ABOUT THE AUTHOR

STEVE MARX HAS BEEN SELLING, HELPING SALESPEOPLE, and consulting on the development of sales organizations for nearly his entire career. He conceived and established The Center for Sales Strategy (CSS) in 1983 and has led its growth from a one-man shop to today's roster of nearly 30 full-time career staff, building CSS into the media industry's preeminent sales and management consulting and training organization worldwide. Marx created much of the company's original customer-focused selling and talent-focused management systems and training programs, and has led the company successfully into nonmedia B2B sectors. He has helped the company spread its influence throughout the United States and around the world, with clients in Canada, Australia, Malaysia, and Greece.

In 2000, CSS entered the realm of Web-based training through its wholly owned subsidiary, The Center for Online Learning (coLearn). CoLearn's total redevelopment and expansion of the original benchmark CSS workshop *Customer Focused Selling* allows it to make the training available, accessible, and affordable to a wider range of sales organizations the world over. Today, Marx serves as CEO of CSS/coLearn and manages day-to-day operations together with Jim Hopes, president, and John Henley, executive VP.

CSS and coLearn currently provide sales and management consulting and training services to clients worldwide, including benchmark media companies (in radio, television, cable, newspaper, and the Internet) such as Time Warner, Comcast, Cox, Media General, Hearst-Argyle, AutoTrader.com, Bonneville International, Greater Media, Katz, Arbitron, Hubbard, Journal, Dispatch, Emmis, South Central, Federated, Corus (Canada), and Austereo (Australia, Malaysia, Greece).

The company's services have continued to expand from its original base in sales training, and now include management training and consulting; strategic planning; business development conferences and resources; and talent identification, evaluation, and development services. Not surprisingly, CSS has expanded beyond its historic media base and now serves Manheim, the world's largest wholesale vehicle auction company, as well as DMX, a world leader in digital music and visual programming to enhance retail brand image and the shopping experience.

Sales and management practices developed by Marx and CSS have enabled clients to achieve business reputations and revenue market shares that make them the envy of their competitors. Under his leadership, CSS has achieved a client renewal rate unparalleled in media sales consulting; he takes great delight in this extraordinary level of client satisfaction.

Marx is a highly strategic thinker who sets both high ethical standards and high performance standards. He is proud of his record in attracting extraordinarily talented professionals to make their career at CSS over the years, and of the company's very low personnel turnover. Beyond the ranks of CSS employment, Marx has had a strong influence on the personal and professional development of a great many managers and salespeople throughout the world.

Before he founded CSS, Marx was VP/general manager of the radio stations WAAF and WFTQ in Worcester, Mass., for seven years. As a result of his innovation and leadership, the stations reversed their downward trends in audience, service, and reputation, multiplied their revenues nearly tenfold, and moved from red ink to cash cow. He was also a director of the $1.6 billion BankWorcester Corporation and its subsidiary, Worcester County Institution for Savings, and served as a member of its loan workout committee.

In 1979, Marx created Optimum Effective Scheduling (OES) and then developed and enhanced the concept throughout the 1980s. In fact, together with Pierre Bouvard, he wrote the book on OES—literally. *Radio Advertising's Missing Ingredient: The Optimum Effective Scheduling System*, published by The National Association of Broadcasters (NAB) in 1990, became the NAB's best-selling publication of all time, reaching more than 15,000 total sales. OES is widely respected among stations, agencies, and advertisers for its ability to produce superior results—without increasing the ad budget.

Marx received a B.S. in organizational behavior in 1969 from Cornell University in Ithaca, N.Y., where he is involved today in guiding and mentoring the young executives at the University's student-owned-and-operated radio station, WVBR. He was a director and vice president of the Massachusetts Broadcasters Association and a member of the Radio Effectiveness Subcommittee of the Advertising Research Foundation. He was a director of the Worcester Area Chamber of Commerce and served on the city manager's Special Airport Task Force. He has served as a trustee and a vice president at Congregation Schaarai Zedek in Tampa and is an active supporter and volunteer for Academy Prep Center of Tampa, a school expressly for at-risk inner-city kids of middle-school age. But there's still time for fun: Marx is a solo-rated Porsche Club driver at Sebring International Raceway and also enjoys getting his center-console boat up on plane in Tampa Bay.

Marx and his wife Merrill live in Tampa as empty nesters— their son Jeff is a defense consultant in the Washington, D.C. area, and their daughter Emily is a publicist in New York City.

There's more to
The Center for Sales Strategy
than just Interactive Selling!

CSS is focused squarely on *helping organizations develop salesman-agement, salespeople, and sales*. That succinctly stated mission hasn't changed since the company's origin in 1983. The sequence is significant: Sales performance improvement rests on upgrading the practices of each and every *salesperson*...and helping salespeople grow requires that *managers* function in new ways. Short-term programs may hype results in a given quarter, but they leave the organization another 90 days behind in its effort to secure *sustained superiority* in performance.

Strength-based **skill development** trumps the remedial approach every time—fixing weaknesses never produces the turbo-charging impact on sales performance that are routinely achieved by enhancing and leveraging a person's strengths. So CSS helps its clients to elevate the priority for selecting, developing, and retaining the *best talent*; and to install talent-based systems and practices throughout the organization.

Even the best talent needs state-of-the-art selling systems and practices, together with skill training and one-on-one coaching. CSS equips sales managers with essential systems for zeroing in on real customer needs and responding with tailored solutions that add value, distance the threat from competitors, and create the basis for long-term business partnerships.

One size never fits all. We assign CSS Consultants to clients on a long-term basis, so they get to know each organization intimately and tailor systems to each particular environment.

CSS is eager to speak with leaders of sales organizations that (1) sell to other businesses, (2) expect to maintain an ongoing relationship with and to make future sales to its customers, and (3) sell tailored solutions developed from a portfolio of products, services, capabilities, and resources. We want to learn more about your key challenges. Please contact the author at 813.254.2222 or SteveMarx@CSScenter.com, or CSS President Jim Hopes at 813.254.2222 or JimHopes@CSScenter.com.

Bring the One-Day
Interactive Selling
Workshop into your organization!

Your people can learn to Close Like the Pros!

They can learn how to create partnerships from the outset—not by telling their prospects they'd "like to be their partner," but by conducting themselves as partners from the very start. There's no better way of getting partnership behavior back from clients and prospects than to be it, live it, and do it yourself.

You've read the book, so you understand how smoothly *interactive selling* practices can be integrated into the selling system in use at most organizations. Most sales books out there—and most of the sales training workshops you might bring in—prescribe an A-to-Z, bumper-to-bumper, dream-to-done selling system. Adopting their "total plan" requires dumping so much of what has made you so successful to date. *Interactive selling* is different. It's not bumper-to-bumper. For many business-to-business organizations committed to professional selling practices, *interactive selling* adds the one component still missing.

Some of your people are already doing some of these things, consciously or unconsciously. After you've brought the CSS *Interactive Selling* workshop to your people, most of them will be interactive sellers by intent and methodology. They'll know what to do and when to do it—not occasionally or accidentally, but consistently and with purpose. They'll know how to replace *handoff selling* with a full integration of buying and selling, to make the prospect a full partner in the selling phase and themselves a full partner in the buying process. Your sales managers will have a language with which to communicate the entire set of practices...from *contracting expectations* to *mini-closing* to *assigning homework* to *using half-baked ideas* and *trial balloons*.

For more information on the one-day *Interactive Selling*
workshop, please contact the author at 813.254.2222 or
SteveMarx@CSScenter.com, or CSS President Jim Hopes at
813.254.2222 or JimHopes@CSScenter.com.